Ray Mi

HOUSTON

SECOND EDITION

Ray Miller's HOUSTON

SECOND EDITION

T 77655

Gulf Publishing Company
Houston, Texas

Ray Miller's Houston
Second Edition

Gulf Publishing Company
Book Division
P.O. Box 2608, Houston, Texas 77252-2608

10 9 8 7 6 5 4 3 2 1

Library of Congress Cataloging-in-Publication Data

Miller, Ray, 1919-
    [Houston]
    Ray Miller's Houston. — 2nd ed.
      p   cm.
    Includes bibliographical references (p.   ) and index.
    ISBN 0-88415-081-X (hbk). — ISBN 0-88415-080-1 (pbk)
    1. Houston (Tex.)   I. Title.   II. Title: Houston.
F394.H857M54   1992
976.4'235—dc20   92-10731
                                                      CIP

Contents

Foreword viii

Introduction ix

PART ONE: **Early History 1836 - 1899** 1

PART TWO: **Houston 1900 - 1946** 47

PART THREE: **Development Since World War II** 101

PART FOUR: **Color Photographs** 187

Listings

> Mayors of Houston, 208
> County Judges, Harris County, 209
> Harris County Representatives, U.S. Congress, 210
> Municipalities Wholly or Partly in Harris County, 211
> School Districts in Harris County, 212
> Colleges and Universities in Houston/Harris County, 213

Sources 214

Index 217

For Gray and Geoff

Foreword

(written for the original edition, 1982)

It has been my privilege to know Ray Miller and to follow his career from the time he was a fledgling reporter. He has escalated to great heights in his profession. More than once I have heard young radio and television reporters refer to him as their idol.

Instead of retiring to an easy life of inactivity when he completed his tenure with KPRC, he chose to visit many parts of Texas to record and report on some of the unique glories of our state. He is owed much for perpetuating in his *Eyes of Texas Travel Guides* these captivating, historical sagas.

Now in this volume, Mr. Miller returns to the city of his love — a city he has seen grow, develop and prosper. There is no one better qualified to give us the overview contained in this book, and to furnish an insight into Houston as it has been and is, than this gifted author.

Leon Jaworski

Introduction

People come to Houston now from everywhere and for all kinds of reasons. Time was when most of the people moving to Houston came from the smaller cities and often with the idea of moving on later to a bigger city. This idea is not as prevalent or as valid as it was. The list of cities bigger than Houston is considerably reduced. The list of liveable bigger cities is very, very short.

I moved here in 1940 because Jack McGrew offered me a better job at KPRC Radio than the job I had at KFJZ in Fort Worth. I accepted the offer without ever really thinking about whether I wanted to live in Houston. I assumed I would get better offers later and move on to bigger places. But I never got a better offer; never found a place I would rather live.

Ray Miller
Houston
1992

PART ONE

Early History
1836-1899

"The town of Houston is located at a point on the river which must ever command the trade of the largest and richest portion of Texas . . ."

Excerpt from the founders' original advertisement.

Architect Philip Johnson has said that Houston is the last great 19th century city where people are not afraid to try anything. Douglas Milburn called it the "Last American City" in the book he wrote about it. Whether it is either or neither of these, Houston started as a scheme to make money. John Kirby Allen and his brother Augustus were looking for land they could sell for more than they had to pay for it when they came up Buffalo Bayou in the summer of 1836. The imprint of that beginning is likely to be part of Houston's character forever. But an imprint is not necessarily a stigma.

Texas had been Spanish territory for 300 years when Moses Austin in 1821 persuaded the Spanish to let him bring in some Anglo settlers from the United States. Moses Austin died and Spain lost control of the territory shortly after that, but Moses's son negotiated a new deal with the new Mexican government. Buffalo Bayou was on the eastern edge of the colony Stephen F. Austin developed. The land where Houston started was granted to John Austin.

Relations between Mexican authorities and the Anglo colonists never became really cordial. Mexican colonial policies and attitudes changed several times as the Mexican government changed. Some of the colonists resented the way they were treated. Some of the Mexicans resented the presence of outsiders. The Mexican government was trying to limit further Anglo immigration by the early 1830s. Some of the Anglo colonists were agitating for a separate state government.

Texas had agents in the United States by 1835 enlisting volunteers to fight against Mexico. Volunteers without any legal status were coming in, looking for action. They were the original illegal aliens in Texas. Davy Crockett and some others went to San Antonio and joined the little garrison in the Alamo after Texans seized it from the Mexicans in December, 1835. Mexican authorities realized that they were losing control, so Mexican President Antonio Lopez de Santa Anna gathered up an army and headed for Texas. He was determined to put down the rebellion and more. He planned to chase all the Anglos out of Texas.

1) Houstonians almost never refer to their town as the "Bayou City." This is a term put in circulation by writers and it is seldom used by anybody else. A bayou is a short stream on the gulf coast that would be called a creek if it were some-where else. A bayou in Louisiana usually is called a BY-YOU. A bayou in Texas usually is called a BY-OH. But you may hear the word pronounced either way here. Some historians claim our bayou was named for the buffalo fish. But it probably was named for the buffalo. The stream is labeled Buffalo River on some early maps. It is not big enough to be a river. But Buffalo Bayou has been Houston's biggest asset from the beginning. It is the reason the city is here.

Santa Anna was in San Antonio preparing to attack the Alamo when 59 people met at Washington-on-the-Brazos to sign a document declaring Texas free and independent. They all said they were Texans, but only two of the people there on March 2, 1836, had been born in Texas. Some others were bona fide settlers. Some had been in Texas as long as 10 years, but several had been in Texas less than a year. Sixteen of the signers had come from Tennessee. Sam Houston and several of the other signers from Tennessee had been friends and political allies of President Andrew Jackson there. Everybody knew Jackson wanted to expand the United States to the west. Many people believe the separation of Texas from Mexico was a Washington idea.

Santa Anna's Mexicans overwhelmed the Alamo garrison on March 6 and started eastward. They looted and burned homes and villages to terrorize the settlers. The settlers fled with what possessions they could carry. Sam Houston and his Texas Army maneuvered to stay out of the way of the advancing Mexican columns. Santa Anna had things going his way. He heard that the interim government of Texas was at Harrisburg on Buffalo Bayou. He headed for Harrisburg to try to capture the rebel leaders. The Texas officials got away from Harrisburg just in time. The Mexicans burned Harrisburg and, on April 16, they looted the homes along the bayou and around Morgan's Point.

Sam Houston and the Texas Army showed up in the same vicinity. The Texans and Mexicans selected camp sites within sight of each other

2) John Kirby Allen was a member of the first congress of the Republic of Texas. He died before the town he and his brother founded was two years old. John died at 29. Houston Library.

3) Augustus C. Allen was John Allen's older brother. The Allen brothers had come to Texas in 1832. They established the city of Houston shortly after the Battle of San Jacinto in 1836. Augustus Allen withdrew from the Allen enterprises in 1850 and left Houston. He died in Washington in 1864. He is buried in New York. Houston Library.

4) John Allen is buried in Founders' Cemetery on West Dallas near downtown Houston. This cemetery was beyond the city limits on the road to San Felipe when it was established.

5) The Allens were New Yorkers. The whole family moved here after John and Augustus established the town. Their mother and father and four older brothers were living in Houston by the time John died.

6) The land the Allens chose for their town site was part of the original Stephen F. Austin colony. Austin's was the first Anglo colony in Texas sanctioned by the government of Mexico. Houston Library.

4

2

3

4

JOHN KIRBY
ALLEN

BORN IN CANASAREAUGH, NEW YORK
1810 · · · CAME TO TEXAS IN 1832 ·
DIED IN HOUSTON AUGUST 18, 1838

Erected by the State of Texas
1936

5

6

on the plain that has been called the San Jacinto Battleground ever since. Santa Anna was satisfied the war was over. He had the rebel government and all the settlers on the run. He had the enemy army in a position where he could attack any time he wanted. He apparently thought he deserved a little break. The Mexican president may have been relaxing in his fancy campaign tent with a young woman named Emily Morgan at midafternoon on April 21 when Sam Houston and the Texas Army stormed into his camp and put an end to the war and the Mexican rule over Texas. Emily Morgan was a mulatto servant in Col. James Morgan's house at Morgan's Point. Santa Anna's troops had taken her prisoner a few days before the battle. She never got any official credit for whatever role she played at San Jacinto, but she is remembered in the folk song "The Yellow Rose of Texas."

The principal settlements in what is now Harris County before the Battle of San Jacinto were Harrisburg, Lynchburg, New Washington, and New Kentucky. Harrisburg, Lynchburg, and New Washington were all on Buffalo Bayou. New Kentucky was inland near the present town of Tomball. Harrisburg was an important port. Supplies for the Austin colony came to Harrisburg by ship and then were hauled by ox cart to San Felipe and other inland settlements. Houston did not exist.

John and Augustus Allen were New Yorkers. They had come to Texas in 1832 to speculate in land and land claims. The Allens apparently were the first to realize what an opportunity Santa Anna had created when he burned Harrisburg. The new republic needed a port. The Allens made an offer for what was left of Harrisburg, but there were problems with the title. So they rented a boat and sailed up Buffalo Bayou looking for another likely site. They were taken with the land around the junction of White Oak Bayou and Buffalo Bayou. It was the John Austin grant. Austin had died. Augustus Allen bought 2,000 acres on the south bank of the bayou from his widow. The Allens hired Gail Borden to lay out the townsite. Borden is the man Houstonians can thank for the wide streets downtown. The founders named several of the streets for heroes of the revolution and named the town for the winner of the Battle of San Jacinto. The Allens had decided that their new port should also be the capital of the new republic.

There were some other contenders for the capital, but the Allens had some advantages. The man they named their town for was elected president of the republic a short time later. John Allen won a seat in congress at the same election in September, 1836, and also got appointed to President Houston's staff. The brothers and their colleague Robert Wilson were able to persuade the president and the congress that the new republic

6

7) The Battle of San Jacinto was fought around the western approach to Lynch's Ferry. Nathaniel Lynch established the ferry service here in 1822. The boats are different, but the Lynchburg Ferry operating today follows approximately the same course across the San Jacinto River just below the mouth of Buffalo Bayou. The service is operated now by Harris County Precinct 2 and it is free.

should put its capitol in the town named for Sam Houston. The congress made the decision at the temporary capital at Columbia on November 30, 1836.

Robert "Honest Bob" Wilson had been elected to the senate. He evidently advanced the Allens' cause by sharing with President Houston some of the real estate he earned by assisting the Allen brothers. Houston wound up with 12 lots in the new town. The Allens' records indicate the lots were paid for. Houston told people they were given to him. He gave several of them away. He gave one to a sailor he had never seen before. The occasion was the ceremony in Houston marking the first anniversary of the Battle of San Jacinto. Marquis James wrote in "The Raven" that the Lone Star flag got tangled in its halyard so that it was not waving properly from the flagpole. A sailor from the visiting schooner *Rolla* climbed the pole and straightened the flag. The president called him over when he got back down and gave him the piece of property.

Houston never was a frontier town. There were substantial settlements much farther west long before Houston was established. But it certainly was a primitive town when it became the capital of the Republic of Texas. One visitor described it as a city of tents with no more than a couple of frame buildings. One of the frame buildings was the capitol building the Allen brothers build at the corner of Main and Texas. The

7

Allens promised the government free use of this building as long as the government remained in Houston.

President Houston's residence was a log cabin a few blocks away. It had two rooms and a lean-to at the back. Naturalist John James Audubon visited the new capital shortly after it was established and someone took him to meet the president. Audubon later wrote that President Houston and Surgeon General Ashbel Smith were sharing one of the cluttered rooms in the official residence and the president's two black servants were living in the lean-to. The president was not complaining. He wrote in 1838 that Houston had improved more than any place he knew anything about. He said new people were moving in at the rate of 200 a month.

The advertising the Allen brothers did alleged that ships could sail from New Orleans or New York to Houston without obstacles. Many people doubted this claim; so the Allens staged a demonstration. They engaged the captain of the steamboat *Laura* to make a trip from Columbia to Houston in January, 1837, and they invited several distinguished Texans to ride along. The *Laura* was the smallest steamboat in Texas waters at the time; she was just 89 feet long. The *Laura* took three days to travel from Harrisburg to Houston. The distinguished passengers were called upon several times to help clear away logs and obstructions, but several steamboats were making regular trips to Houston within a year after that demonstration.

8) Mexican President Antonio Lopez de Santa Anna brought an army to Texas in the early spring of 1836 to drive all the Anglo colonists out. He had decided they never were going to make satisfactory Mexican citizens. Santa Anna recaptured the Alamo and San Antonio but he was surprised, defeated, and taken prisoner at San Jacinto on the outskirts of the present city of Houston less than two months later. Houston Library.

9) Santa Anna was not devoting his full attention to the campaign when the Texas Army swarmed into his camp on the afternoon of April 21, 1836. It is not part of the official record, but the gossip has always been that the president was closeted with a new female acquaintance in his tent, about where this marker now stands in the San Jacinto Battleground State Park.

10) Former Tennessee Governor Sam Houston commanded the Texas forces at San Jacinto. His troops wanted Santa Anna killed because the Mexican Army had executed captured Texan soldiers at Goliad. Houston considered it better strategy to keep Santa Anna as a hostage to ensure the withdrawal of the three or four thousand Mexican troops still in Texas. Houston was wounded at the Battle of San Jacinto but he recovered in time to be elected first president of the new republic in the fall of 1836. Houston Library.

9
8

10

THE ORIGINAL PLAN OF HOUSTON

11) The Allen brothers named their new town for Sam Houston as part of their campaign to get the government of the republic to make the town its headquarters. A Congress Square was provided in the original plan of Houston, executed by Gail Borden. Congress Square became Market Square after the government moved away. Gail Borden went on to found the Borden Milk Company. Houston Library.

12) The government of the Republic of Texas moved to Houston in the spring of 1837 and conducted its business until 1839 in a building owned by the Allen brothers. The Allens charged no rent. They regained control of the building and rented it to a hotel operator after the government moved to Austin. Houston Library.

John Kirby Allen died in 1838. Augustus and his wife, Charlotte, split up in 1850 and Augustus left Texas for good. He died in the East in 1864. Charlotte stayed and dominated Houston society for 45 years. The original Allen promotional fever had infected the four other Allen brothers and enough other early Houston settlers to ensure that Houston would survive.

Houston had two two-story houses, a warehouse, and a hotel by the end of 1837. One of the two-story houses was the A. C. Briscoe home at Main and Prairie. Briscoe was a veteran of the Battle of San Jacinto and the first county judge here. The first warehouse was at Main and Commerce, backing up to the bayou. The first hotel was at Travis and Franklin where the Southern Pacific building is now. The hotel was built by Ben Fort Smith and operated by George Wilson.

Harrisburg had been the original administrative center of Harris County. The town was founded in 1824 by John Richardson Harris. The county was originally called Harrisburg County. The county seat was moved to Houston shortly after Houston was established. The name of the county was then changed to Harris. The first courthouse in Houston was a double log cabin and the original jail was a crude log building with no windows or doors. There was only a trap door in the roof. The original courthouse and jail were on the same block where the Harris County Civil Courthouse is today.

One of the capital city's prominent female citizens was locked up in the log jail and put on trial for her life in the log courthouse in 1839. Pamelia Mann had borrowed some money from a man named Hardy to finance a boarding house at Washington-on-the-Brazos during the convention that produced the Texas Declaration of Independence. Hardy

12

11

13

13) *Charlotte Allen had a disagreement with her husband, Augustus, over the division of the family's assets after John Allen died. They separated. Augustus moved away. Charlotte stayed. She lived at Main and Rusk and was a pillar of the community until she died in 1895. Houston Library.*

died and his widow demanded that the money be repaid to her. Pamelia produced a receipt purporting to show that she had repaid most of the loan before Hardy died. The widow denounced the receipt as a forgery and filed charges.

Pamelia Mann had built another boarding house by the time the case came to trial. She was operating the Mansion House at Congress and Milam. She was kept in jail during the trial because of the seriousness of the charge against her.

Forged land titles were among the most serious problems Texans had to deal with during the early days of the republic. The first Congress of the Republic accordingly had passed a law making forgery a capital offense. The penalty was hanging. The jury found Pamelia Mann guilty of forging the receipt. The jury recommended mercy, but the judge followed the law and sentenced Mrs. Mann to death. The jury petitioned President Mirabeau Lamar to commute the sentence. He did more than commute it; Lamar issued a presidential pardon to Mrs. Mann and she went back to her boarding house.

Saving Pamelia Mann from the hangman was about the last official act Mirabeau Lamar performed as president in Houston. Lamar was the son of a Georgia planter. He came to Texas in 1835. He performed heroically the duties Sam Houston assigned him at the Battle of San Jacinto and was elected vice president when Houston was elected president in 1836.

Opponents and critics of Sam Houston rallied around Lamar in the second presidential election in 1838. Houston could not run because the constitution prohibited a president from serving consecutive terms. Peter W. Grayson, James Collinsworth, and Robert Wilson lined up against Lamar. The Houston partisans favored Grayson but he shot himself before

14) Charlotte was buried in the Allen family plot in Glenwood Cemetery on Washington Avenue. This cemetery was established in the 1830s. Members of many of the city's pioneer families are buried here.

14

election day and Collinsworth jumped off a boat into Galveston Bay and drowned. Lamar defeated Wilson handily and took office in December, 1838.

The new administration declared war on the Indians, threatened the Mexicans, and started looking for ways to get the government out of the town named for Sam Houston. Lamar wanted to move the capital to a site on the Colorado and he got the congress to go along with him. The government hired contractors to build a new town and named it for Stephen F. Austin.

The Allen brothers put a sign in the window of the old capitol building in Houston, offering it for rent. It was vacant about a month before it was rented and turned into a hotel. The Capitol Hotel operated in the original capitol building until 1881 when Abraham Groesbeeck bought it and tore it down. He built a new brick hotel in its place and gave it the same name. Groesbeeck went broke and William Marsh Rice bought the new hotel at a tax sale. Rice had come to Texas from Massachusetts in 1838 with a little money he had made from a store he owned there. Rice settled in Houston in 1839 and opened a store. He prospered and became one of Houston's richest and most prominent citizens.

13

Houston had several permanent buildings, a school, and a couple of theaters by this time, but some people thought the town was bound to die after the government moved away. Andrew Briscoe thought Harrisburg had better prospects, so he moved there. An outbreak of yellow fever discouraged people from moving to Houston and a couple of wrecked ships blocked the bayou between Houston and Harrisburg but the town never came close to dying. Merchants and shippers formed the Buffalo Bayou Company to raise money to pay for removal of the sunken ships and other obstacles from the bayou. Business leaders got the congress to

15

16

OLD HARRISBURG

EARLY TEXAS PORT AND TRADING POST, SITE OF STATE'S
FIRST STEAM SAWMILL, GRIST MILL, RAILROAD TERMINAL.
TOWN FOUNDED, 1826, BY JOHN R. HARRIS, WHO WAS FIRST
SETTLER IN 1823. BECAME SHIPPING CENTER FOR EARLY
COLONIES, ESTABLISHED WHEN TEXAS WAS PART OF MEXICO,
WITH BOATS CARRYING CARGO TO AND FROM TEXAS PORTS
AND POINTS IN THE UNITED STATES AND MEXICO.

BECAME THE SEAT OF GOVERNMENT OF THE REPUBLIC
OF TEXAS, MARCH 22–APRIL 13, 1836, WHEN DAVID G. BURNET,
PRESIDENT OF THE AD INTERIM GOVERNMENT, AND SEVERAL
OF HIS CABINET, RESIDED NEAR HERE IN THE HOME OF
MRS. JANE HARRIS (SITE MARKED), WIDOW OF TOWN FOUNDER.
HERE PRESIDENT BURNET ADOPTED THE FLAG FOR THE
TEXAS NAVY IN 1835. LOCAL RESIDENT, MRS. SARAH DODSON,
HAD MADE HERE THE FIRST TRI-COLOR LONE STAR FLAG.

GENERAL SANTA ANNA ATTACKED THE TOWN WITH 750
MEXICAN SOLDIERS ON APRIL 16 ATTEMPTING TO CAPTURE
BURNET AND HIS CABINET. THE WHOLE TOWN WAS BURNED.

AFTER TEXAS GAINED ITS INDEPENDENCE AT NEARBY
SAN JACINTO, THE TOWN WAS REBUILT AND AGAIN THRIVED.
THE BUFFALO BAYOU, BRAZOS AND COLORADO, FIRST RAIL-
ROAD IN TEXAS, BEGAN HERE IN 1852. DURING THE CIVIL
WAR MADE THE TOWN A CONFEDERATE RAIL CENTER.
BECAME A PART OF HOUSTON, BY ANNEXATION, IN 1926

17

18

15) The government of the republic bought a small store building at Main and Preston and converted it into a residence for the chief executive in 1838. This first Texas White House was on the site where the Scanlan sisters later built the Scanlan Building. Houston Library.

16) The first shopping center in Houston looked something like this. The Harris County Heritage Society's shops on Bagby Street occupy a frame building designed to resemble the row of commercial establishments originally built in 1837 on the west side of Main Street between Preston and Congress.

17) The Harrisburg section of east Houston was a town before Houston was. John R. Harris settled here in 1823. The town of Harrisburg was named for him and the county was originally called Harrisburg County. Some of the early history of Harrisburg is recorded on this marker at Broadway and Lawndale.

18) The constitution of the republic did not allow consecutive terms for the president so Texans had to choose a new president when Sam Houston's first term ended in 1838. Houston did what he could to prevent it, but Mirabeau B. Lamar was elected president. Lamar's administration moved the government to Austin. Houston Library.

grant them a charter for a chamber of commerce to promote the city and the port.

There was some question about the legality of the Buffalo Bayou Company's moving of sunken ships since they were private property. Congress cleared up the question in 1842 by granting Houston specific authority to have disabled ships and other obstructions moved out of the channel. The congress at the same time granted the city the right to levy charges on shipping to raise money for improvements to the channel.

Houstonians now began forming churches. The First Methodist was organized first. The Allen brothers donated half a block of land for it on Texas Avenue where the Houston Chronicle Building is today. The First Presbyterian congregation met in the capitol building until the Presbyterian Church was built at Main and Capitol in 1842. The Episcopalians organized a church in 1839, but they didn't build their first building at Texas and Fannin until 1845. The First Baptist Church was organized in 1841 with its original building at Texas and Travis. The first Catholic church acquired a site at Franklin and Caroline in 1841.

The principal newspaper was the *Telegraph and Texas Register*. Gail Borden and his brother Thomas started the paper in San Felipe in 1835. They moved it to Harrisburg during the panic in 1836. Mexican troops seized the press in Harrisburg and threw it into the bayou. The *Telegraph and Texas Register* suspended publication until the Bordens could get another press. The Bordens resumed publication in Columbia in time to cover the first meeting of the Congress of the Republic there. The Bordens sold their paper to Jacob Cruger and Francis Moore when the government of the republic left Columbia. The new owners brought the paper to Houston, where they stayed when the government moved on to Austin.

The *Telegraph and Texas Register* changed hands several times and went out of business in 1873. A new owner revived it as the *Houston Telegraph* in 1874, but it closed down for good in 1878. The *Telegraph and Texas Register* was not the first Texas newspaper, but it was the first one to publish more than just a few issues.

The government of the republic moved back to Houston briefly in 1842. Sam Houston had been elected president again and he never favored Austin as the capital. The Mexicans made a couple of forays into San Antonio and President Houston used those as an excuse to close down Austin. The old capitol building at Texas and Main was a hotel by this time; so the Senate had to meet in the Odd Fellows' Hall. The House met in the new First Presbyterian Church at Main and Capitol until the government moved on to Washington-on-the-Brazos. It stayed there until Texas joined the Union in 1845.

16

Houston had organized a city government with a mayor and eight aldermen by 1840. The city was divided into four wards. Each ward elected two aldermen. The First Ward was everything north of Congress and west of Main. The Second Ward was everything north of Congress and east of Main. The Third Ward was everything south of Congress and east of Main. The Fourth Ward was south of Congress and west of Main. The Fifth Ward and Sixth Ward were added later as development spread north of Buffalo Bayou. The wards ceased to exist as political subdivisions many years ago, but the terms sometimes are still used.

Stage lines linked Houston with Austin, Richmond, and Washington-on-the-Brazos by the early 1840s. The first cotton compress was established in 1844. The first sawmill was established on Buffalo Bayou at Milam Street about the same time. A cornmeal mill on the bayou at Texas Avenue was using three oxen on a treadmill for power. The city extended from the bayou on the north to Walker Street on the south, from Bagby on the west to Caroline on the east, in 1842. The city limits were extended a little later to cover nine square miles. English writer William Bollaert observed that Houstonians all slept under mosquito bars in the summers because the mosquitoes were so bad.

19) *One of Houston's pioneer merchants and businessmen founded the school that became Rice University. William Marsh Rice came here in 1838. He was living in New York when some of his associates, bent on taking for themselves the money he had earmarked for the school, killed him. Rice University.*

19

The 1850 Census was the first one after Texas joined the Union. It showed Houston's population as 2,397. Galveston was the biggest city in the state and the port there was getting most of the business Houston coveted. Most ships could not make it over the sand bars to get into Buffalo Bayou. They stopped at the Galveston docks or else unloaded their cargoes onto barges. Only barges and small ships were calling at Houston.

The legislature appropriated money for the first time in 1853 for improvements to the Houston channel. The appropriation was only $4,000. But the lawmakers voted another $45,000 in 1857 to cut channels through Redfish Reef and Clopper's Bar to allow bigger ships to enter the Houston channel. Most of the boats operating in the Houston channel at that time were owned by the Houston Navigation Company. The company was a syndicate of Houston businessmen including William Marsh Rice. Houston Navigation charged $2 or $3 a head for passengers and 50 cents a bale for cotton.

William Marsh Rice was one of the leading citizens in Houston by this time. He and Ebenezer Nichols had one of the biggest stores on Main Street. Rice got interested in railroads after he married railroad promoter Paul Bremond's daughter Margaret in 1850. The first railroad was the line the Buffalo Bayou, Brazos and Colorado built from Harrisburg

21

22

20) A few copies of early editions of the Telegraph Texas Register are preserved in libraries and private collections. This was the principal newspaper in Texas during the revolution and for some time afterward. Houston Library.

21) Episcopalians have been worshipping at the corner of Texas and Fannin since Texas was a republic. The first Episcopal congregation was organized in 1939. The present Christ Church Cathedral was built in 1893.

22) The Annunciation Catholic Church at Crawford and Texas was built in 1874. The steeple, added in 1881, was designed by the great Galveston architect Nicholas Clayton.

to Stafford in 1853. Rice had stock in it and he also invested in Bremond's Houston and Texas Central in 1856.

The Lutherans organized their first Houston church in 1851 and the first iron foundry began making kettles for the sugar plantations.

The city of Houston acquired its own dredge boat in 1856 and put it to work on the bayou. Sixty thousand bales of Texas cotton went to market in 1858 through the Port of Houston.

The Census of 1860 credited Houston with a population of 4,845. Fourteen Texas counties had more people than Harris County. The richest man in the county was William Marsh Rice and he was believed to be the second richest man in the state. Rice owned the biggest building in Houston. One of his several businesses was hauling ice to Houston from New England by ship.

The first rail line between Houston and Galveston was completed in 1860. A telegraph link between the two cities had been completed a short time earlier. The telegraph line was kept operating all during the Civil War with sulphur water from Sour Lake. The batteries normally used sulphuric acid. None was available in Texas during the war because of the Union blockade, but some one discovered that the smelly water from Sour Lake made a reasonable substitute. Five short rail lines operated out of Houston by the time the Civil War began.

The 1860 Census also showed a total of 1,068 slaves in Houston. All were not owned by planters. William Marsh Rice owned 15 of them. Most of the people in the city at that time came from the Old South. Sentiment here was strongly in favor of secession. The vote in Harris County in February of 1861 was 1,084 for secession and 144 against.

Houston abolished all wharf charges just before the war started, trying to draw business away from the Port of Galveston. There was substantial traffic between the two ports during the war, but very little between them and points beyond because of the federal blockade. Blockade runners made big profits from cargoes they managed to slip past the Union ships. Some of the blockade runners operated out of Houston. One of them was owned by merchant T. W. House. He was the father of Edward M. House, later to be assistant to President Woodrow Wilson.

Sam Houston was governor of Texas in 1861. He did everything he could to prevent secession, short of calling in the Union Army. President Abraham Lincoln sent word that such a call would be answered. Houston decided to try to prevail through reason, but it was not a time for reason. The Secession Convention of 1861 swept Houston out of office when he failed to appear to take the oath of allegiance to the Confederacy that the Convention had decided to require. Houston told everybody

23

23) The Sisters of the Incarnate Word
established the Incarnate Word Academy
at Annunciation Church in 1874. Nicholas Clayton designed this building for the
school in 1906.

24) Annunciation Church owns the old
W. L. Foley home at 704 Chenevert.
Foley immigrated from Ireland and
established the W. L. Foley dry goods
company in the 200 block of Travis in
1870. Foley Brothers, established by his
nephews, James and Pat Foley, survives
today as Foley's. W. L. Foley Company
closed in 1950. W. L. Foley's daughter
Blanche left the home to the church when
she died in 1965. The proportions are
unusual because the second floor had to
be lowered when the Foleys moved the
house to this location in 1909. It stood
originally on part of the site where the
Union Station was built in 1910. This
was an upper class residential neighborhood in the late 19th Century.

24

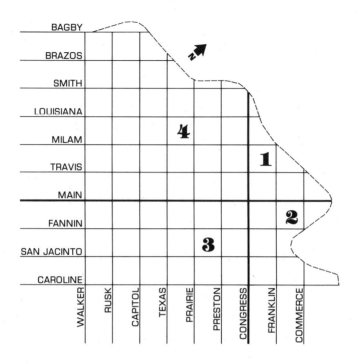

BAGBY
BRAZOS
SMITH
LOUISIANA
MILAM
TRAVIS
MAIN
FANNIN
SAN JACINTO
CAROLINE

WALKER RUSK CAPITOL TEXAS PRAIRIE PRESTON CONGRESS FRANKLIN COMMERCE

4 **1** **2** **3**

25

25) *The original political organization of Houston had the city divided into four wards. Each ward was entitled to two aldermen in the original arrangement. Houston Library.*

willing to listen that the South could not win the war. Other Texans were killed by vigilantes and bushwackers for making statements like that, but people seemed to think Sam Houston had earned the right to say anything he wanted to say and do anything he wanted to do. Sam Houston thought so, too. Confederate authorities put out an order at one stage during the war requiring all Texans to carry identification. Houston did not and would not do it. People said that a patrol stopped Sam Houston one day and asked for his identification. Houston supposedly bellowed that San Jacinto was his passport and he supposedly rode on without any further interference. It may have happened. It may have been a story somebody else started or it may have been a story Houston started. But it sounded to Texans like something Sam Houston might do. More people were beginning to believe Houston's predictions about the outcome of the war by the time he died in 1863.

Houstonians volunteered for Confederate forces as eagerly as they voted for secession. One thousand men turned out on September 9, 1861, to join Benjamin F. Terry in the cavalry regiment that became known as Terry's Texas Rangers. The Bayou City Guards, the Gentry Volunteers, the Houston Artillery, and the Texas Greys were some of the other Confederate units recruited in Houston. Houston bartender Dick Dowling became an instant hero by commanding a little Confederate force that routed a Union invasion force at Sabine Pass on September 8, 1863. There was no fighting in the immediate vicinity of Houston. The closest was in Galveston. A force of Union soldiers and sailors captured the island city in December, 1862. A couple of Houston steamboats were recruited for the makeshift task force Confederate General John B. Magruder organized to take the island back on New Year's Day, 1863. There were no more Union troops in Galveston until the occupation army arrived on June 18, 1865. Houston was occupied the following day by the 114th Ohio Regiment and the 34th Iowa Regiment.

A major outbreak of yellow fever in 1867 killed Dick Dowling in Houston, occupation commander Charles Griffin in Galveston, and many others in both cities.

The process the North called "Reconstruction" was proceeding fairly uneventfully until 1867 when the U.S. Congress threw out the presidential plan for reassimilating the Southern states and put in its own, much harsher Reconstruction program. The U.S. military governor of Texas removed the elected governor from office and arranged a new election. Union veteran Edmund J. Davis was chosen governor. He removed most local officials and replaced them with people loyal to the Union. Houston's elected Mayor Alexander McGowen was removed and replaced by Joseph Morris and then by T. H. Scanlan. Four elected aldermen were removed and replaced with black Unionists.

Many freed slaves had moved to Houston. Most of them settled in what they called Freedmantown on the outer edge of the Fourth Ward.

B. A. Shepherd and T. M. Bagby organized the First National Bank in 1866. The Houston Gas and Fuel Company was established in 1866 to make gas from coal. The first gas lights were installed in 1868. The first trolley cars appeared on Houston streets in 1868. They were pulled by mules. The city's first ice plant opened in 1869.

Galveston got the lion's share of the maritime business when ships started running regularly again. Galveston would continue to be the dominant port into the 1920s and grow very rich while Houston struggled to overcome its natural disadvantages. Houston businessmen in 1869 formed the Buffalo Bayou Ship Channel Company to dredge the channel to a depth of nine feet.

The Congress of the United States agreed in 1870 to designate Houston a port. The Census of 1870 gave Houston a population of 9,332. Harris County had a population of 17,375. Only Washington County had more people.

The population of Galveston in 1870 was 13,818 and the Port of Galveston was doing much more business than the Port of Houston. But the only rail line between Galveston and the mainland passed through Houston. Shipments between Galveston and the interior were subject to handling charges in Houston and they sometimes were held up by quarantines. Galveston bankers and merchants established the Gulf, Colorado, and Santa Fe Railroad Company to build a line into the interior that passed to the west of Houston through Sugarland. Business at the Port of Galveston got even better but cotton farmers were beginning to grumble about freight charges and about the wharf rates on the island.

Congregation Beth Israel established the first synagogue in Houston, at Franklin and Crawford, in 1870. The City Bank of Houston opened the same year and closed in 1885.

Congress approved $10,000 for improvements to the Houston Ship Channel in 1872. The Buffalo Bayou Ship Channel Company had started

26) The founders intended from the beginning to make Houston a major seaport. But Houston is 50 miles from the sea. Ships of any size reached the Houston docks only with great difficulty in the early years. Houstonians started improving the channel in the 1840s. The improvements have been continuing ever since. Houston Library.

27) The former home of William Marsh Rice is one of the historic buildings the Harris County Heritage Society maintains in Sam Houston Park on Bagby. Rice's business partner Ebenezer Nichols was building this house when Rice and Margaret Bremond married in 1850. The Rices bought the building from Nichols and lived in it until Margaret died in 1863. The house originally stood on the courthouse square. It was moved to another location by subsequent owners, then moved here and restored. The Heritage Society conducts tours of the restored buildings in this park.

28

29

26

30

dredging a channel across Morgan's Point, but the work was interrupted by the financial panic of 1873.

Mayor Scanlan and his Reconstruction regime decided to tear down the old Houston City Hall and put up a new city hall and opera house on the same site. They annexed several additional miles of territory to get the tax base to support a bond issue. The original plans called for a building to cost $250,000. Overruns and miscalculations brought the total to more than $400,000. The new building was insured for only $100,000 when it burned in 1876. The insurance company made some repairs, but the building burned again a few years later. Scanlan was gone from the mayor's office long before that. The Reconstruction period ended in Texas in 1874 when Richard Coke won the governor's office from Edmund J. Davis. Coke put people of the old school back in office in the cities. He appointed James T. D. Wilson to succeed T. H. Scanlan as mayor of Houston. Wilson was the son of the pioneer politico and Allen brothers associate Robert "Honest Bob" Wilson. The city had a debt of $1.4 million and no credit rating when Scanlan left office in 1874. The city's bond holders were growing restless.

Houston got through rail service to St. Louis in 1873 when the Houston and Texas Central linked up with the Missouri, Kansas, and Texas at Denison.

28) Houston's plan to turn Buffalo Bayou into a major port centered mostly on the cotton trade in the beginning. Planters with access to the Brazos River sent their cotton to Galveston by barge and steamer. Planters in the area north of Houston sent their cotton to Houston brokers by wagon and oxcart. It was loaded onto barges and carried down to the bay where it was usually loaded directly onto ships, bypassing the Galveston docks. The roads between Houston and the cotton country were so awful that Houston boosters hatched a plan to pave them with planks. That plan was abandoned when Paul Bremond started building the Houston and Texas Central Railroad into the cotton belt in the 1850s. Houston Library.

29) The earliest railroad in Texas was the Buffalo Bayou, Brazos, and Colorado between Harrisburg and Stafford. The first locomotive was named the General Sherman. It was named for General Sidney Sherman. He was a hero of the Battle of San Jacinto and the founder of the Buffalo Bayou, Brazos, and Colorado. Houston Library.

30) T. W. House was one of the most prominent businessmen in Houston before and during the Civil War. He was a merchant and also a planter and he had some success at running ships through the Union blockade during the war. House was the first person to produce and sell ice cream in Houston. Houston Library.

The Houston Light Guard was organized in 1873 to compete in military events. There had been two similar volunteer groups before the Civil War. Both had disbanded as their members joined various fighting units for the war. The Houston Light Guard fought as a unit in the Spanish-American War and then was incorporated into the Texas National Guard before World War I.

The leading cotton brokers and a few businessmen met on June 12, 1874, to form the Houston Board of Trade and Cotton Exchange. C. S. Longcope was elected president. The board reorganized in 1877 as the Houston Cotton Exchange and Board of Trade.

The Port of Galveston and the Morgan Steamship Line fell out over wharf fees in 1874. Galveston had not been charging this good customer any fees before and Charles Morgan was very displeased when fees were imposed. Morgan had earlier dredged his own channel and created the Port of Morgan City because of a similar move by the Port of New Orleans. He decided to deal the same way with the Port of Galveston.

Morgan acquired control of the Buffalo Bayou Ship Channel Company by agreeing to finish the cut through Morgan's Point and dredge a 9-foot channel up Buffalo Bayou to Sims Bayou. He completed this and estab-

31) This monument in Glenwood Cemetery marks the grave of one of the first Texans to fight for the South in the Civil War. Benjamin F. Terry was a planter in Fort Bend County. He voted for secession as a delegate to the Secession Convention in Austin in 1861 and then went immediately to Virginia to fight in the first Battle of Manassas. Terry returned to Houston after the battle to recruit the cavalry unit that took the name Terry's Texas Rangers. Terry was killed while leading the Rangers in their first battle in December, 1861. Houston Library.

32) Towns and counties and schools all over the South were named for Confederate heroes after the war. The name used most often was that of the Confederate President Jefferson Davis. Houston and Harris County gave his name to the public hospital they built on Elder Street in 1924.

lished a terminal he called Clinton in 1876. Morgan built a rail line to connect his docks at Clinton with the major railroads in Houston. He had a port he could use without paying wharf fees to anyone and he was soon collecting fees from the owners of other ships using his channel across Morgan's Point. Congress approved $75,000 for more improvements to the Houston channel in 1876. The first grain elevator was established on the channel the following year. The Port of Houston was gaining ground at the expense of the Port of Galveston.

Harris County had several free public schools by 1873. The first free public schools were established in Houston in 1877. They were segregated and administered by the city government.

A state fair was held in Houston each year between 1871 and 1878. The fairgrounds were west of South Main between Hadley and Elgin. The Houston Light Guard formed the guard of honor when former Confederate President Jeff Davis visited the fair in 1875. The fairground site was subdivided after the show was discontinued. The present state fair in Dallas began in 1886.

Mayor Wilson and the city council gave a private contractor a franchise to build a water system for Houston in 1878. Residents had depended upon shallow wells and cisterns up to that time. The contractor built a dam on Buffalo Bayou at Preston and a pipeline system to deliver bayou water to homes and business buildings. There were complaints about the taste and color of the water almost from the start. A few citizens drilled deeper wells and found good artesian water. The franchise holder got

SACRED TO THE MEMORY OF
THIRTY TWO
CONFEDERATE SOLDIERS
HO DIED IN THEIR COUNTRY'S SERVICE
REST IN PEACE.

33

33) *That first Jeff Davis Hospital was built on the site of an old city cemetery where several Confederate veterans had been buried. Repair shops for the fire department have since been built on the same property right alongside a marble slab the city installed in 1924 to atone for disturbing the veterans' graves.*

34) *The Ancient Order of Hibernians commissioned this memorial to a Confederate veteran from County Galway. Richard W. "Dick" Dowling was a saloonkeeper in Houston before and after the Civil War. He was a lieutenant in the Confederate Army during the war. He gained fame by thwarting a Union attempt to invade Texas through Sabine Pass. Dowling Street was named for him. This statue was placed originally in Market Square, moved to Sam Houston Park, and then to Hermann Park.*

34

30

35) The Union army of occupation
removed from office in 1867 all public
officials involved in any way with the
Confederate cause. More "reliable"
people were put in their places. New
officials and speculators from the North
were called "carpetbaggers" by the South-
erners because many had come from the
North with only what possessions they
could carry in a carpetbag. T. H. Scanlan
was the man the Union people chose to
be mayor. Scanlan had lived in Houston
before the war. He spent the war years
in Mexico. He was therefore not a "carpet-
bagger" but to old Houstonians he was
the "carpetbag" mayor. Scanlan was
mayor until Reconstruction ended.
Houston Library.

35

36) Local military organizations were not allowed during the Union occupation but as occupation forces were withdrawn several such groups were organized. The Houston Light Guard was established in 1873 to take part in drills and parades and to fight when called upon. They won a lot of prizes and trophies and built this armory in 1925 at Caroline and Truxillo. The building was donated to the Texas National Guard in 1939. It was abandoned and put up for sale in 1990.

37) The Morgan Steamship Line took exception to the wharf rates in Galveston in the 1870s and built a new terminal at Clinton on Buffalo Bayou. The Morgan Company also deepened the channel up to this point. Morgan ships connected here with Morgan's rail line, later acquired by the Southern Pacific. Little remains of Clinton except a dilapidated dock.

36

37

38

38) *The first building built by the Houston Cotton Exchange and Board of Trade is still in use. It was built in 1884 at the corner of Franklin and Travis. The building was restored in 1973.*

discouraged and put the Houston Water Works up for sale. A group headed by former mayor T. H. Scanlan bought the system. The new owners drilled some wells and tried to deliver only well water to households, but the bayou water they were furnishing to industries and the fire hydrants kept getting mixed with the good water. The city bought the system in 1906, drilled more wells and stopped taking water from the bayou.

Several other Texas counties grew more between 1870 and 1880 than Harris County did. The Census of 1880 showed a population of 16,513 for Houston and 27,985 for Harris County. Grayson, Dallas, Bexar and Fayette counties all had larger populations than Harris County.

The first telephone exchange was installed in Houston in 1880. There were 50 telephones in the city. Long distance service didn't begin until 1895.

39) *Telephones looked like this when Houston got its first telephone exchange in 1880. The button at the top set off a bell to get the operator's attention. The receiver was also the transmitter. Courtesy Southwestern Bell.*

40) *The company that became Houston Lighting and Power was founded in 1882. Electric streetlights began to replace gas lights in 1884. This oil-burning generator at the Gable Street plant was photographed about 1900. Courtesy Houston Lighting and Power.*

41) *A new hotel was built in 1881 on the site where the capitol building had stood. This brick building at Texas and Main was being called the Capitol Hotel when William Marsh Rice bought it, and he kept that name. The trustees of his estate changed the name to Rice Hotel after Rice was murdered. Houston Library.*

39

The rail link between Houston and New Orleans was completed in 1880. Rail service between Houston and the West Coast began in 1882.

Congress made further appropriations for improvements to the Houston Ship Channel in 1880, 1881, and 1882, but Galveston continued to be the leading port. Houston and Galveston both were using quarantines by this time to divert business away from each other. The ostensible reason for the quarantines was yellow fever. All the coastal areas had outbreaks fairly regularly. Dr. Carlos Finlay of Cuba first suggested in 1881 that the fever was spread by the *Aedes Aegypti* mosquito. But residents of the Gulf Coast consumed tons more quinine before a U.S. Army Commission headed by Dr. Walter Reed finally proved the mosquito theory in 1900 and started to develop control measures.

The Houston Electric Light and Power Company was established in 1882 and the first street lights were turned on in 1884. The Houston Gas Light Company took over Houston Electric Light and Power in 1887 and sold it to Citizens' Electric Light and Power Company in 1891. Citizens' went into receivership in 1898 and was reorganized as Houston Lighting and Power Company in 1901.

34

42) The Sisters of Charity of the Incarnate Word established the first general hospital in Houston in 1887. St. Joseph's Infirmary had 40 beds. It was the forerunner of the present St. Joseph's Hospital complex. Courtesy St. Joseph's Hospital.

43) The first paving project in Houston was not a city project. The merchants in the two blocks of Main Street nearest the bayou put up the money to have these two blocks paved with cut limestone. Houston Library.

44) The Sweeney-Coombs Building at Main and Congress was built in 1889. It housed various businesses until Harris County bought this entire block in the 1970s as the site for the Harris County Administration Building. All the buildings were demolished except this one at the corner of Congress and Main and the one at the corner of Congress and Fannin. The Sweeney-Coombs Building was restored to house some of the county offices.

44

More than 20 newspapers started publishing in Houston between 1865 and 1880. Most of them lasted only a short time. A paper called *The Houston Post* began publishing in 1880 and folded in 1884. The present *Houston Post* was born in 1885 when the morning *Chronicle* and the evening *Journal* combined and took the name *Houston Post*. Ross Sterling bought this paper in 1924. He merged it with the *Houston Dispatch* and published it as the *Houston Post Dispatch*. Sterling sold the paper to J. E. Josey in the 1930s. Josey changed the name back to *Houston Post*. Former governor William P. Hobby bought controlling interest in the *Post* in 1939. His heirs sold the paper in 1983 to the *Toronto Sun*.

45

45) The Pillot Building at Congress and Fannin fell down almost completely before it was restored in 1990 to house a cafe and offices. Eugene Pillot built this building in 1858. It is the last iron-front commercial building in Houston.

46) John Henry Kirby was one of the first people to exploit the East Texas pine forests. He founded the Kirby Lumber Company and the Kirby Petroleum Company. Houston Library.

47) Kirby moved to Houston in 1890 and bought a big Victorian frame house at Smith and Gray. Kirby remodelled the house and turned it into the brick and stone mansion that still stands on the site. Kirby was a Democrat and some of the strategy for the 1928 Democratic National Convention was worked out in meetings in this house.

46

47

W. H. Bailey started the *Houston Herald* in 1884. Marcellus E. Foster started publishing the *Houston Chronicle* in 1901. Foster bought the *Herald* in 1902 and published a combined paper he called the *Houston Chronicle and Herald*. The name was shortened to *Houston Chronicle* and Foster traded a half interest in the paper to Jesse Jones in 1908 as part payment for the building Jones built for the *Chronicle* that year. Jones bought out Foster's remaining interest in 1926 and continued to publish the *Chronicle* until he died in 1956. Houston has had only two daily papers, the *Post* and the *Chronicle*, since 1964 when the *Chronicle* bought out the *Houston Press* and shut it down. E. W. Scripps had established the *Press* in 1911.

The Southern Pacific established shops and a regional headquarters in Houston in 1886. The Commercial National Bank opened the same year and merged with the South Texas National in 1912. The Houston National Bank opened in 1889. It was reorganized in 1909 as the Houston National Exchange Bank.

The mayors of Houston during the 1880s were W. R. Baker and D. C. Smith. They managed to work out a compromise settlement with the investors holding the bonds the city's Reconstruction administration had issued. The city's voters set the stage for the compromise by voting to pay the holders of those bonds no more than 50 cents on the dollar. The investors came out a little better than that in the final settlement and the city's credit rating began to improve.

Some fancy steamboats were operating on Buffalo Bayou between Houston and Galveston by this time. The *Diana* and the *T.M. Bagby* were described as floating palaces equal to anything operating on the Mississippi.

The Sisters of Charity of the Incarnate Word opened the first hospital in Houston at Franklin and Caroline in 1887.

48

48) The first electric streetcars were a big improvement over the old mule cars but the early models did not offer much protection from the weather. San Jacinto Museum of History, Cecil Thompson Collection.

49) The five-story Kiam Building was a showplace when it was finished in 1893. It was built for Kiam's Clothiers. Sakowitz occupied this building from 1918 until 1928. The Kiam Building had the first electric elevator in town.

50) The corner of Main and Texas was one of the busiest intersections in town when Jacob Binz built this distinguished office building in 1894. This was the first six-story building in Houston. It still stands but it has been remodelled and five floors have been added. Courtesy Spaw-Glass Co.

49

The Census of 1890 gave Texas a population of more than two million. Seven counties had more people than Harris County. Houston was credited with 27,557. Galveston had 29,084.

Congress started spending substantial sums of money on the Port of Galveston in the 1890s. There was an appropriation of $6 million to pay for the jetties at the channel entrance. These were just as helpful to Houston traffic as they were to Galveston traffic. But the congress also put up money to deepen the channel to the Galveston docks. The channel was dredged down to 14 feet in 1893, to 18 feet in 1895 and then to 25 feet in 1896. Most ships could steam right up to the docks. It was a big plus for Galveston.

Retiring Congressman J. C. Hutcheson of Houston proposed a survey for a 25-foot channel to Houston. Representative Thomas Ball succeeded Hutcheson and wangled an appointment to the Committee on Rivers and Harbors. Ball got the 25-foot channel for Houston approved. But congress made only token appropriations until the great hurricane of 1900 raised questions about the viability of the Port of Galveston.

50

51

51) Part of the old 1890s Magnolia Brewery has been turned into a restaurant. The brewery included an ice plant and occupied several buildings around the intersection of Franklin and Milam. The brewery buildings extended out into and across Buffalo Bayou. Some of the old brickwork is still visible under the Franklin Street bridge.

52) Sam Houston Park where the Heritage Society's old houses are now was the original Houston city park and for a long time the only one. Houston Library.

52

53) Jesse Holman Jones moved to Houston from Dallas in 1899. He went into the lumber business, then into building, then into banking and real estate, and became the most influential citizen in town. *Houston Library.*

53

After Charles Morgan died, the federal government in 1890 bought the Morgan channel across Morgan's Point and eliminated the tolls. It was a plus for Houston but the bigger ships still had to stop at Galveston. The Southern Pacific acquired Morgan's rail line and the docks at Clinton, after Morgan died.

John Henry Kirby moved to Houston from Tyler County in 1890. Kirby was a lawyer. He won some cases for forest owners and then went into the timber business himself, on a big scale. Kirby was the richest man in Houston by 1900.

Nebraska banker O. M. Carter came to Houston in 1890 and bought up the two trolley systems then operating in the city. The cars were still being drawn by mules but Carter changed that. He consolidated the lines, formed the Houston City Street Railway Company, and put electric trolleys in service in 1891. This made it possible for Carter to promise and deliver trolley service to Houston Heights, started the same year by Carter and the Omaha and South Texas Land Company. Twelve rail lines were operating in and out of the city by this time and Houston was the most important rail center in the state.

The city had several packing houses and manufacturing plants by 1894. Barbed wire, brick, tile, cigars, textiles, carriages, wagons, and beer were some of the products being made in Houston.

43

Jacob Binz put up the first skyscraper in 1894 at the corner of Main and Texas. The Binz building was six stories tall.

The city's merchants and businessmen formed the Houston Business League in 1895 and this organization became the Houston Chamber of Commerce in 1910. The first city park was established in 1899. This was Sam Houston Park, bound by Bagby, Walker, and Dallas, where the Harris County Heritage Society's old houses are now. There was a small zoo when this was the only park in the city.

Jesse H. Jones moved to Houston in 1899 to manage a branch of his uncle's M. T. Jones Lumber Company. The Joneses had come to Texas from Tennessee when Jesse was nine. They settled in Dallas in 1883. What might have happened if Jesse Jones had stayed in Dallas can only be guessed at, but he became a legend in Houston. He opened his own lumber business shortly after arriving in Houston. That led him into building and that led him into banking. He became the biggest booster of the city and the port. Jones did more to advance Houston's causes than any other single individual from the time he arrived until his death.

Jesse Jones believed in Houston and real estate. He was associated with many rich and famous oilmen, but he was always dubious about their business. Jones invested $20,000 in the Humble Company when it was founded. He was pleased to be able to sell the stock and get out a year later. He doubled his money, but some other early stockholders made large fortunes as Humble grew and evolved into the giant Exxon USA.

55

54) South Main Street was lined with elaborate homes at the turn of the century. T. H. Scanlan and his spinster daughters lived in this one until the daughters dismantled it and used the materials to build another home on their plantation in Fort Bend County. Houston Library.

55) The home built for lawyer R. S. Lovett at 2017 South Main stood until the 1940s. There is a McDonald's on this corner now. The McDonald chain bought out a local hamburger business with the same name to get the right to do business as McDonald's in Houston. Houston Library.

PART TWO

Houston
1900-1946

"Houston is booming. It is a live town. The commercial instinct
is very strong."

John Millsaps, 1910

The official population of Houston reached 44,633 in the Census of 1900, passing Galveston. Harris County had a total population of 63,786. Dallas and Bexar counties both had bigger numbers.

Houstonians had 2,000 telephones in service in 1900. The Houston and Texas Central Railroad built the Grand Central depot that year off Washington Avenue where the main post office is today.

The Carnegie Foundation gave the city $50,000 for a library building. The city provided the site at McKinney and Travis. The new Houston Lyceum and Carnegie Association took over the small library that had been accumulated by the Houston Lyceum, established in 1848. The first librarian in the new building was Julia Ideson.

The San Jacinto Chapter of the Daughters of the Republic of Texas was organized in 1901 to take care of the San Jacinto Battleground and put up markers. The battleground was the property of a widow named Peggy McCormick when the battle was fought. The property was sold to various individuals after Mrs. McCormick died. The state bought 10 acres of the site in 1883 and bought 200 more acres in 1891. Smaller tracts have been added since then. The San Jacinto Battleground Historical Park now covers about 400 acres.

The Stone and Webster Company took over the city's transit system in 1901 and continued as the operator after ownership passed to the Galveston-Houston Corporation in 1910.

The oil discoveries at Spindletop in 1901, at Humble in 1905, and at Goose Creek in 1906 put Houston on the way to becoming the center of the oil and oil field equipment businesses. Two of the drillers active in southeast Texas after the Spindletop discovery were Howard R. Hughes and Walter Sharp. They became impatient with the drill bits they had to work with. Hughes perfected a bit that would cut through rock better than anything drillers had been able to get before. He and Sharp established the Sharp-Hughes Tool Company in Houston to manufacture the new bit. Hughes bought Sharp's interest after Sharp died in 1912. He ran the business as Hughes Tool Company until he died in 1924. It passed, then, to Howard R. Hughes, Jr.

1) Major oil strikes were being made all around Houston in the early 1900s. There were no rules on spacing or proration. The oilmen crowded their wells as close together as possible here in the Humble Field and in all the other areas where they were finding oil.

2) Steel tycoon Andrew Carnegie's estate gave Houston a library building. Carnegie had specified his money was to be used for buildings. Books were never included. Luckily, Houston had some books. The Carnegie Library stood at the corner of Travis and McKinney. Woolworth's occupies the site now. Houston Library.

3) Houston started the 20th Century with a new railroad passenger depot. Grand Central Station was near the site, off Washington Avenue, where the Southern Pacific (Amtrak) Station is now. Houston Library.

4) The city built the fire department a fancy new central station in 1902 at the corner of Texas and San Jacinto. Organized firefighting had started in Houston in 1838 when Congress issued a charter to a volunteer bucket brigade organized by the citizens. The firefighters were all volunteers until 1895 when they went on the city payroll. The department's last three fire horses were retired when the firemen moved from this building to a new central station at Caroline and Preston in 1924. The retired horses were stabled at Hermann Park Zoo and a firefighter went there to feed them every day until the last one died. Courtesy Houston Fire Department.

3

4

J. S. Cullinan moved the Texas Company from Beaumont to Houston in 1908. Cullinan's was the biggest name in the oil business in Texas. He became a big booster of the city and the port and did as much as anybody to focus the oil business on Houston.

Congress appropriated another million dollars for the ship channel in 1902. The turning basin was completed in 1908.

Automobiles appeared in a Houston parade for the first time in 1902. G. W. Hawkins started selling Oldsmobiles at 903 Texas Avenue. Hawkins was the original holder of Texas Motor Vehicle License Number

5

5) The Perfecto Dry Cleaning plant on Fannin looks like a church for a very good reason. The congregation of the Tuam Avenue Baptist Church built the building in 1904. Perfecto bought it in 1920 when the congregation left to establish the South Main Baptist Church.

6) The noted Prohibitionist Carry Nation came to Houston in 1905 to wreck a local saloon with her axe. She was living in Kansas at the time, but Carry was no stranger to Houston. She and her husband had lived in Columbia and Richmond. He was a reporter for the Houston Post for a time. Houston Library.

7) The saloon Carry Nation wrecked was in this building on North San Jacinto. The proprietor had named the saloon for her and she was offended. There was a second floor here in 1905 but it was removed following a fire.

One. He gave it up in 1914 because Governor Jim Ferguson thought he should have it and it has been assigned to the governor's office ever since.

The Houston Golf Club organized in 1903 and built the city's first golf course on the south bank of Buffalo Bayou just west of downtown. The club reorganized as the Houston Country Club in 1908 with William Marsh Rice II as president and moved to South Wayside Drive.

Houston voters in 1904 approved an experiment with the commission form of government. The government was headed by a full-time mayor. Each of the four aldermen headed one of the city departments. H. Baldwin Rice was the first mayor to serve under this arrangement. He was a nephew of William Marsh Rice.

Carry Nation appeared in Houston in 1905 and did about $750 worth of damage to a saloon in the Fifth Ward. Carry was the most famous prohibitionist in the country. Her specialty was attacking saloons with an axe. She took her axe to the establishment in the Fifth Ward because the proprietor was calling his place the Carry Nation Saloon.

6

7

There were 80 automobiles on the streets of Houston by 1905. That was the year young Oscar F. Holcombe moved to Houston from Alabama. Holcombe went into the construction and contracting business and prospered. He ran for mayor in 1920. He was elected and he served as mayor of Houston off and on for the next 35 years. Holcombe served a total of 11 terms.

The Union National Bank was formed in 1905 when the Union Bank and Trust and the Merchants' National merged. The Lumbermen's National Bank opened in 1907. Bankers' Trust opened in 1908 with Jesse Jones as chairman. The Great Southern Insurance Company was founded the following year. W. W. Baldwin came from Iowa in 1908 to found the town of Bellaire. He started a trolley line in 1909 to connect his town with Houston.

The Houston population was up to 78,800 in the 1910 Census. The population of the county was 115,693. Dallas and Bexar counties still had more people.

8

9

The Union Railroad Station opened in 1910 and made the corner of Texas and Crawford one of the busiest spots in town.

Congress voted in 1910 to approve a Houston proposal for completing and maintaining the Houston Ship Channel. A delegation of citizens had visited Washington in 1909 to suggest that Houston and the U.S. government split the cost.

The Texas legislature authorized creation of a navigation district and the district put a proposal for a bond issue to a public vote. City and county voters approved an issue of $1.4 million to deepen the channel to 25 feet. Investors were not enthusiastic about buying the bonds but Jesse Jones rounded up the leading Houston bankers and convinced them

10

8) Joseph S. Cullinan moved his Texas Company to Houston in 1908. Cullinan had started the company that would become Texaco in Beaumont in 1903. He was one of the first people to grasp the vision of a petroleum center here and he became a big booster of the city and the ship channel. *Houston Library.*

9) Joseph Cullinan donated the land the Museum of Fine Arts stands on. The site is a triangle at the junction of Montrose and South Main. Cullinan bought it from the George Hermann Estate.

10) Cullinan also bought a large tract of land along the west side of South Main Street, south of the museum site and created here the most exclusive subdivision in Houston history. He never offered any of the big lots in Shadyside subdivision for sale to the public. He sold them only to his friends and associates. He and several other early oil millionaires built homes here.

11) *Former Mayor T. H. Scanlan left his spinster daughters very well fixed when he died. The Scanlan sisters spent part of their legacy for an office building they regarded as a monument to him. The Scanlan Building was the finest in town when it was completed in 1909 at the corner of Main and Preston where Sam Houston once lived.*

12) *The Southern Pacific Railroad was one of the biggest employers in town in 1910 when the railroad built this hospital at 2015 Thomas Street for S. P. employees. The railroad got out of the hospital business years ago and this building is now an AIDS clinic.*

11

the Houston banks had a moral obligation to buy those bonds. Several arrangements for managing the port were tried before the city and the county agreed on the present Port of Houston Authority. There are five commissioners. The city names two, the county names two, and the city and county jointly choose the chairman.

Houston had 15 miles of electric streetcar lines by 1910, and 190 miles of paved streets. Electric interurban cars began running between Houston and Galveston when the new causeway was completed in 1911. There were 18 cars a day. The tracks followed the route of the present Gulf Freeway. The trip took about an hour each way. The service continued until 1936 when it was scrapped because most people by then were traveling in their own cars.

The Rice Institute started classes in September, 1912. This was the school that became Rice University. It was provided for in a will William Marsh Rice wrote before he was killed in New York in 1900. Legal complications delayed the building of the school. Rice's second wife had written a separate will before she died, purporting to give to others some of the property she and Rice had set aside for the school. Also a New York lawyer had forged a will purporting to give him most of the property Rice had set aside for the institute. That lawyer eventually was convicted of influencing an associate to kill Rice with chloroform. That ended the lawyer's claim. The trustees Rice had designated to manage his estate and his institute made a settlement with the second Mrs. Rice's heirs. They had about $4.5 million in assets left for the institute, including the Capitol Hotel. They changed the name of the Capitol to Rice Hotel and leased it to Jesse Jones. He demolished the building and put up a new Rice Hotel. It opened in 1913.

One of the original Rice trustees was Rice's lawyer, James A. Baker. He got most of the credit for exposing the New York lawyer's plot and

for holding the Rice estate together. He was the son of one of the founders of the Baker and Botts law firm and the grandfather of President Bush's secretary of state, James A. Baker III.

The United States built a new post office building in Houston in 1912. This building in the 700 block of San Jacinto is now called the U.S. Customs House. The main post office moved to a new building off Washington Avenue in 1961.

The Houston Symphony Orchestra was founded in 1913. It has been directed at different times since then by such luminaries as Leopold Stokowski, Sir John Barbirolli, Andre Previn, and Christoph Eschenbach.

The 25-foot-deep channel to the turning basin was completed in 1914. President Woodrow Wilson took part in the dedication on November 10. The president pressed a button in Washington that set off a cannon at the port. But ships were not lined up waiting to get into the Houston Ship Channel. The war in Europe had reduced ocean commerce drastically. But Houstonians were able to persuade the Southern Steamship Company to schedule regular service between Houston and New York. This called for another celebration. A Deep Water Jubilee was arranged to coincide with the expected arrival of the Southern Steamship Com-

13

14

13) An electric interurban train ran between downtown Houston and downtown Galveston for 25 years, beginning in 1911. Most people were convinced by the time the service was abandoned in 1936 that the automobile was the only way to go. San Jacinto Museum of History, Cecil Thompson Collection, courtesy Houston Public Library.

14) E. W. Scripps established the Houston Press in 1911 and the paper usually had some of the best writers in town until the Scripps-Howard chain sold it to the Houston Chronicle in 1964. The Chronicle shut the Press down. Author Thomas Thompson was once city editor at the Press. He has died and the building at Rusk and Chartres has been demolished since this picture was made in 1982.

15

16

15) This building on San Jacinto is now called the U.S. Customs Building. It was built in 1912 to house the Houston Main Post Office. Generations of recruits and draftees passed though the Armed Forces Induction Center here.

16) A few conscientious objectors passed this way, too. It was at the Induction Center on San Jacinto that heavyweight champion Mohammed Ali declined in 1966 to be drafted for the war in Vietnam. The Supreme Court recognized Ali's objector status in 1971. Houston Chronicle.

17) The original buildings on the Rice campus on South Main were completed in 1912. William Marsh Rice provided the money but he was murdered in New York in 1900 and his killers tried to make off with the fortune he had willed to the school.

pany's steamer *Satilla*. There would have been free barbecue and a lot of speeches at the turning basin if the *Satilla* had arrived when she was supposed to on August 19, 1915. But the ship was delayed in the Gulf by the great 1915 hurricane. About 2,000 people turned out to welcome the *Satilla* when she did arrive on August 22, but it was not the jubilee it was meant to be.

Oil companies soon began shopping for refinery sites along the channel. Petroleum Refining Company had a refinery in operation and Sinclair had one under construction by 1918.

The Texas Company completed a new headquarters building on Rusk between Fannin and San Jacinto in 1914. J. S. Cullinan left the Texas Company and established the American Republics Oil Company.

George Hermann died in the fall of 1914. He was a bachelor with no close relatives. Houston was his beneficiary. George Hermann's parents had come to Houston sometime in the late 1830s. He told people they arrived with $5. His mother pawned her jewelry to raise money to start a bakery and the Hermanns prospered. George inherited substantial real estate. He bought more land and some of the land he bought turned out to have oil under it. He grew rich but not extravagant. Shortly before he died, George Hermann gave the city 285 acres of land off South Main where he had once operated a sawmill. That gift was the nucleus of Hermann Park. The city built the first public golf course there in 1915. George Hermann also left the city the downtown block where the City Hall Reflection Pool is now. He left the balance of his estate in a foundation to build and maintain a hospital. Hermann Hospital opened in 1925.

The Anderson Clayton Company of Oklahoma put a branch office in Houston in 1907. The company had been founded by Frank and M. D.

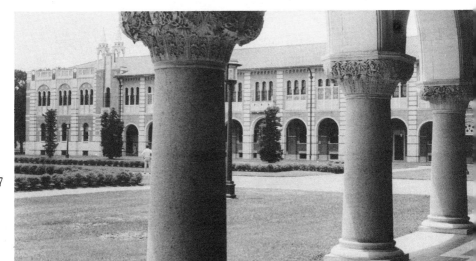

Anderson and Ben and Will Clayton. They were cotton brokers. They brought their headquarters to Houston in 1916 and became the biggest cotton dealers in the world.

J. S. Cullinan in 1916 gave the Houston Art League the money to buy a tract of land at Montrose and South Main for a museum. The Museum of Fine Arts was established on that site in 1924. The Art League had started in 1900 as the Houston Public School Art League.

James A. Elkins moved to Houston from Huntsville in 1917. He served as district attorney briefly during World War I. Elkins started a law practice after the war with William Vinson and went in with J. W. Keeland in a bank that eventually became First City.

Ross and Frank Sterling had established the Humble Oil Company in 1911. They and several other independent operators combined in 1917 to create Humble Oil and Refining Company. Ross Sterling was the first president. The other officers and directors were W. S. Farish, H. C. Wiess, R. L. Blaffer, W. W. Fondren, C. B. Goddard, L. A. Carlton, Frank Sterling, and banker Jesse Jones.

The residents of Houston Heights agreed in 1918 to be annexed to the city of Houston. The Heights had incorporated in 1896.

18

The U.S. Army established two training bases in Houston for World War I. Ellington Field trained pilots and bombardiers. It was named for one of the air age's early casualties, Lieutenant Eric Ellington. Camp Logan was a National Guard base. The army established it as a training center for guardsmen being sent to France. A regular army unit was brought in from the border to guard the base while it was being built. The enlisted men in this unit were all black and they resented the rigid segregation practiced in Houston.

City police arrested one of the black privates on August 23, 1917. The police said the private interfered in another arrest they were making.

18) Jesse Jones started his career in the lumber business and then went into building and banking. He built the Rice Hotel in 1913 partly because he wanted a nice place to live downtown. Jones never built a home. Houston Library.

19) George Hermann left a large estate and no heirs when he died in 1914. He directed the trustees of his estate to create a hospital to care for the needy. Houston Library.

20) Hermann Hospital was completed in 1925 adjacent to what would become the Texas Medical Center. It is the teaching hospital for the University of Texas Medical School and a pioneer in helicopter ambulance service.

19

20

21

A black M.P. was arrested when he went to the police station to inquire about the case. Both soldiers said they were beaten. The arrests made the black troops angry. Someone started a rumor that a white mob was marching on the base. It was not true, but about 100 black troopers marched out that night looking for a showdown with the police. Some whites armed themselves and went looking for the soldiers. Five policemen and 12 soldiers and civilians were killed. Another 24 people were wounded. Houstonians wanted to lynch the black soldiers. Mayor D. M. Moody got control of the situation by getting a declaration of martial law and a force of Coast Guardsmen from Galveston and soldiers from San Antonio to patrol the city.

The Army court-martialed 63 black soldiers. Thirteen were hanged. The others were sentenced to death or life in prison, but most were eventually released.

Houston and the rest of the country were caught up in the great experiment with Prohibition as the 1920s began. The Gulf Coast was well suited to rum-running and there was never any shortage of intoxicants in Houston during the Prohibition era. Serious drinkers took precautions, though, in case the new law turned out to be enforceable.

Howard R. Hughes invested in booze some of the money he made from drill bits. Noah Dietrich wrote in *Howard, The Amazing Mr. Hughes* that the senior Hughes bought all the stock of the Rice Hotel bar when the bar closed June 25, 1918. The liquor was moved to the Hughes home on Yoakum and Howard, Jr. inherited what was left of it when his father died in 1924. Young Hughes put Noah Dietrich in charge of his Houston interests when he moved to Hollywood to make movies and discover new starlets. Dietrich said in his book that it became his duty to smuggle the Hughes booze to California. It was not illegal for Hughes to have the liquor for his own use, but it was illegal to transport it from one

64

22

23

21) Houston business and civic leaders subscribed for a long time to the Allen brothers' original idea that the place for the port was here at the foot of Main Street. When the Army Engineers were made responsible for the channel they determined that the head of it and the turning basin should be downstream, much closer to old Harrisburg than to the original Port of Houston. Houston Library.

22) It has been a long time since ships called at the foot of Main Street. The original port area was landscaped and turned into Allen's Landing Park in the 1970s.

23) Regular steamship service did not begin until 9 months after the port was completed. Business improved after the steamship Satilla made her first visit in 1915. Houston Library.

24

25

place to another. Dietrich said he succeeded in shipping it by railroad, disguised as movie film. No one questioned it because everybody knew Howard Hughes was making movies.

Dr. Oscar Norsworthy in 1919 transferred to the Texas Conference of the Methodist Episcopal Church, South, the small hospital he had established in 1908 at San Jacinto and Rosalie. This was the beginning of Methodist Hospital. The original trustees included W. W. Fondren, Will Clayton, James A. Elkins, and Jim West.

The 1920 Census placed the population of Houston at 138,276. The city was ranked 45th in the nation. The population of the county was 186,667. Dallas and Bexar counties still had more people.

The city installed the first traffic signals in 1921. They were metal "Stop" and "Go" signs that had to be operated by hand. George Fuermann of the *Houston Post* wrote that Houston was the second city in the country to get such signals, after New York. The manual signals were replaced by automatic signals in 1927.

Leopold Meyer and others organized the Community Chest in 1922. Clarence Wharton was the first president. The name of the agency was changed to United Fund in 1951 and then to United Way in 1979.

26

24) Business was depressed for the first few years after the port opened because World War I disrupted maritime business. The army built a major base south of the city to train flyers for that war. Ellington Field came back to life in World War II. National Guard jets still fly from here but the city now owns Ellington. Houston Library.

25) The planes the students flew at Ellington in World War I were primitive. The army hadn't even owned an airplane until 1910. Houston Library.

26) Camp Logan was established on the western edge of the city in 1917 to train soldiers. The army stationed some black troops here while the base was being built. Friction developed between the black soldiers and Houston police. Some of the black soldiers armed themselves the night of August 23 and marched into town shooting at whites. Police and armed citizens fired back. Seventeen people were killed in what was called the Camp Logan riot.

Mike and Will Hogg bought Camp Logan after the war, to turn it into a subdivision. Catherine Emmott and Ilona Benda started a campaign to save part of the base as a park, to be a memorial to the soldiers of World War I. The Hoggs agreed to sell the property to the city and it became Memorial Park. Houston Library.

27) Oscar Holcombe, center, was elected to his first term as mayor of Houston in 1920. He had come to Houston from Alabama to start a career as a construction contractor and it led him into politics. He served more terms as mayor than anyone else, before or since, but the Houston climate never agreed with him. Holcombe had hay fever. He could not sleep in Houston in the summer, before air-conditioning. He tried to spend most of the summer at his retreat in Hunt. If he had to be in Houston in the summer, he drove to Galveston every night and checked into the Buccaneer Hotel on the seawall where the air was cleaner. Houston Library.

28) Parking space was already getting scarce in downtown Houston in the 1920s. This is Travis Street, looking north from Texas Avenue. The building in the center background is the Southern Pacific Railroad Building. Houston Library.

27

28

68

29

30

29) American motorists had many domestic makes of automobile to choose from in the early days of motoring and a couple of them were made in Houston. This is a four-cylinder Ranger produced in Houston in the mid-1920s by the Southern Motors Manufacturing Association. It was not a hit.

30) Fords were being assembled in Houston in the 1920s, too. The Ford Company opened an assembly plant in Harrisburg in 1914 and it operated until 1942. The building the assembly plant occupied is now part of the Maxwell House Coffee plant. Maxwell House is a division of General Foods but it was produced first by the Cheek and Neal Company of Nashville and Houston. Maryland Club Coffee was started by the Duncan Coffee Company and sold to Coca Cola in 1967.

31

31) *The River Oaks County Club is the centerpiece in the tightly restricted subdivision developed in the 1920s on what was then the western fringe of Houston. T. W. House III and Tom Ball started this development. Will and Mike Hogg came into it after they sold the Camp Logan property to the city and they and Hugh Potter did most of the development. The clubhouse and many of the original houses have been expanded and updated as property values have increased. This is Houston's Beverly Hills.*

32) *One of the original mansions in River Oaks is owned now by the Museum of Fine Arts. This home was built for the Hogg brothers' sister, Ima Hogg. She called it Bayou Bend and she filled it with fine antiques and lived here for many years before she gave the house and the contents to the museum. Ima and her brothers were the children of James Stephen Hogg, the first native Texan to be elected governor. Hogg served in that office from 1891 to 1895. He made some money in oil and real estate after he left office. A rich oil field was discovered after he died on the Brazoria County plantation he left to Ima and her brothers. They put much of the money into philanthropies and the arts.*

Oscar Holcombe was elected to a second term as mayor of Houston in 1922. He was still talking about the campaign years later. He said his opponents, led by members of the Ku Klux Klan, accused him of being a gambler and a drunk. He was neither, but he knew the charges would trouble his fellow Baptists. He persuaded his pastor to arrange a public trial with a jury of ministers. His accusers put on their case and Holcombe put on his defense and the ministers decided that the mayor was not a gambler or a drunkard. The trial made great publicity. Holcombe was reelected handily and he said he thought every minister on the jury voted for him.

The River Oaks Country Club opened in 1923 in the new River Oaks subdivision on what was then the western edge of the city. T. W. House III and Tom Ball had started River Oaks but Will and Mike Hogg bought in and, with Hugh Potter, did most of the actual development. The Hogg brothers were sons of the late former governor Jim Hogg. They had bought old Camp Logan at the end of WW I intending to put a subdivision there. The first recorded suggestion that some part of the old camp should be preserved as a memorial to the war veterans was made by Catherine Emmott and picked up and publicized by *Houston Chronicle* writer Ilona Benda. The Hoggs accepted the idea and arranged in 1924 to sell to the city the land they had bought at the price they had paid, with a strict prohibition against its being used for anything except park

32

purposes. This provision in the deed has caused the city to reject several propositions from drillers interested in prospecting for oil and gas in Memorial Park, which includes most of what was Camp Logan.

Two more cotton compresses were established on the ship channel by the early 1920s and the Anderson Clayton Company was beginning work on the Long Reach Terminal. Oil field equipment firms were multiplying. Clarence Reed had formed the Reed Roller Bit Company to manufacture a drill bit designed by Granville Humason. H. S. Cameron's ironworks started manufacturing in 1922 a blowout preventer designed by J. S. Abercrombie.

33

34

35

33) Some of the original homes in River
Oaks were fairly modest. But many were
imposing, like this one designed by River
Oaks' favorite architect John Staub for
Hugh Roy and Lillie Cullen in 1933.
Cullen was a descendant of Texas pio-
neers who made a vast fortune in oil and
donated much of it to the University of
Houston and various hospitals. The
Cullen house is now owned by Oscar and
Lynn Wyatt.

34) Less elegant but more famous is the
River Oaks home once occupied by Dr.
John Hill and his wife Joan Robinson Hill.
He was a successful plastic surgeon. She
was a socialite horsewoman. Joan died in
1969. Her rich father Ash Robinson
blamed Dr. Hill. The doctor was tried for
murder but a mistrial was declared. Dr.
Hill was shot to death on the front porch
here in 1972. Authorities considered it a
hired killing. The alleged trigger man was

killed before he could be tried. Two alleged
go-betweens were convicted and sent to
prison but no one was ever charged with
paying for the killing. The Hill case was
the subject of Thomas Thompson's book
Blood and Money.

35) The River Oaks Shopping Center on
West Gray right outside the River Oaks
gates was the first neighborhood shopping
center in Houston. It was looking worn
and tired until the Weingarten Realty
Company restored it in 1980.

36

The Houston School District was established in 1923 to operate the public schools operated up until then by the city. R. B. Cousins was superintendent. The transit system acquired its first buses in 1924.

The city's first licensed commercial radio station went on the air in 1925 with equipment designed and built by Eddie Zimmerman and Alfred Daniel. The station was KPRC; the owner the *Houston Post Dispatch*.

The ship channel was deepened to 30 feet in 1925. The port was ranked 11th in the country in tonnage in 1926. Eight refineries were operating on the channel.

Houston Natural Gas Company started supplying natural gas to Bellaire in 1925. It was piped in from Liveoak County by Houston Pipeline

37

36) *Part of Memorial Park has been preserved in its natural state. Primitive trails wind through the Arboretum section of the park here. Visitors will want to take plenty of insect repellent.*

37) *Ross Sterling was one of Houston's early oil millionaires. He was one of the founders of the Humble Company in 1917 and the first president of Humble. Sterling sold his interest in Humble in 1925. He served one term as governor, 1931-1933, and later founded the Sterling Oil Company. Houston Library.*

38) *Ross Sterling was still president of the Humble Company when the company built the first unit of the Humble Building on Main between Dallas and Polk in 1921. This building became the Main Building when Humble moved in the 1960s to a new building on Bell, now called the Exxon Building.*

38

75

39

39) *Sterling built an extravagant summer house on Galveston Bay at LaPorte. It was said that he told the architect to build him a copy of the White House. The Sterling place is a little smaller than the White House but some of the features are similar. Sterling left the estate to the Optimists' Club to be used as a home for boys, but the optimists eventually sold it.*

40) *Cotton exports increased rapidly through the 1920s and Houston became the leading cotton port in the nation. Houston Library.*

40

Company. The Houston Gas and Fuel Company switched in 1926 from artificial gas to natural gas piped in from Refugio County by Houston Gulf Gas Company. The two companies were soon competing for customers all over the Houston area. Houston Gas and Fuel was absorbed into the United Gas system in 1930 and took the name United Gas in 1936.

The city annexed Harrisburg and the city of Magnolia Park in 1926.

The Southern Motors Manufacturing Association made an automobile called the Ranger Four in Houston for about three years in the 1920s. A company with a similar name made a car called the Dixie here briefly, a few years earlier. Neither car made a hit with the motoring public.

Major new commercial buildings sprouted all over Houston during the building boom of the 1920s. The Humble Building on Main was completed in 1921. This is the building now called the Main Building, between Dallas and Polk. The Warwick Apartment Hotel and the city's Central Library Building were finished in 1926. The Houston Negro Hospital opened at Ennis and Elgin in 1926. It was built on three acres of land donated by the city, with money donated by J. S. Cullinan. This is the hospital now known as Riverside General.

Jesse Jones completed the Lamar Hotel at Main and Lamar in 1927 and he and Mrs. Jones moved there. The Espersons finished the Neils Esperson Building the same year and it was the tallest building in town until Jesse Jones completed his Gulf Building in 1929. The Gulf Building was 35 stories and the tallest building in Houston until well after World War II. But Jones was not an advocate of skyscrapers. He favored zoning and he favored a ten-story limit on commercial buildings. But if other builders were going to build taller buildings, he would build the tallest one. It was not until after he died that a building taller than his Gulf Building was built in Houston.

The Houston Buffs Baseball Stadium was completed in 1928. The Houston team had been established when the Texas League was organized in 1888. The Buffs became a St. Louis Cardinals farm club in 1922. Some of the Buff players went on to fame in the majors: Dizzy Dean, Gus Mancuso, Ducky Medwick, Pepper Martin, and others. A Fingers Furniture Store now occupies the site where the 1928 stadium was and some Buff memorabilia is preserved in the Baseball Museum in the store at 4001 Gulf Freeway.

A new concrete highway to Galveston was placed in service in 1928. Shell Oil started construction of a refinery at Deer Park to be fed by pipelines from West Texas, and in February of 1928 the first airmail plane landed in Houston.

The Democrats agreed to bring their 1928 National Convention to Houston because Jesse Jones guaranteed them a new hall to meet in and

41

some help with the expenses. The convention hall was built at Walker and Bagby within walking distance of Jones' hotels. Franklin Roosevelt came as a delegate from New York to place the name of New York Governor Al Smith in nomination. Young George R. Brown was there to help with details. Roy Hofheinz was there as a page. But it was Jesse Jones' show and the busiest season the Galveston rumrunners ever had.

Chairman Will Hogg and the City Planning Commission filed a report in 1929 recommending that Houston adopt a zoning ordinance but Houstonians were not interested (they voted down zoning proposals in elections in 1949 and 1962).

The U.S. Navy accepted an invitation in 1930 to send the USS Houston here for a visit. The cruiser was the biggest ship to travel the ship channel up to that time. She stayed in Houston a week and Houstonians donated $15,000 to buy a silver service for her wardroom.

Radio Station KTRH began operating March 25, 1930. Jesse Jones was the owner. Ed Bourdon spoke the first words heard on the station.

Houston had passed Galveston in size in 1910. The 1930 Census showed Dallas and San Antonio had been passed, too. The Houston population was listed as 292,352. The city covered 72.2 square miles. It

42

43

41) Clark Gable reputedly took acting lessons in this building in the 400 block of Hyde Park. The building was built in 1927 by drama coach and theatrical producer Frederick Leon Webster.

42) The Democrats held their 1928 national convention in a new stadium especially built for the purpose at Bagby and Walker. New York delegate Franklin D. Roosevelt nominated New York Governor Al Smith for the presidency. Smith lost the election to Herbert Hoover. Roosevelt was elected to Smith's old job as governor of New York.

The first Houston Fat Stock Show and Rodeo was held in this hall in 1932. San Jacinto Museum of History, Cecil Thompson Collection, courtesy Houston Library.

43) The livestock for the first Houston show was borrowed from Emil Marks' LH7 Ranch at Barker, where Marks had been staging rodeos annually since 1920. Courtesy Maudeen Marks.

44

44) Houstonians entertained the crew and bought an elaborate silver service for the wardroom when the cruiser USS Houston visited the port in 1930. Any naval vessel visiting the city it was named for got similar treatment. Port of Houston Authority.

45) A young graduate of Southwest Texas State Teachers' College came to

Houston in 1930 to teach public speaking at Sam Houston High School. Lyndon B. Johnson stayed only one year but he coached the school's debate team to a state championship. He was 22 at the time. President Johnson signed this picture in the school's copy of the 1931 Annual when he was in Houston for a campaign speech in 1964. Courtesy Sam Houston High School.

was the biggest city in Texas and number 27 in the nation. There were 65 industrial plants on the ship channel and 475 manufacturing plants in the county. The channel was deepened to 32 feet in 1932 and to 34 feet in 1935. The rivalry between the ports of Houston and Galveston was still intense, but cotton farmers persuaded the two ports to equalize their rates for handling cotton in 1933.

The Port of Houston was ranked second in the nation in tonnage by 1930. There were 27 tanker lines serving the port, but the Great Depression, reduced foreign demand for U.S. grain, and a port strike all combined to reduce the port's business between 1930 and 1933. There was some gradual improvement after 1933, but the port's business did not reach the level of 1930 again until 1939.

Bank failures were common across the country during the Great Depression of the 1930s. But there was no major bank failure in Houston during that unhappy time. Two major banks were on the point of going under in 1931: Houston National, controlled by Governor Ross Sterling, and Public National, controlled by Odie Seagraves, and W. L. Moody III. Jesse Jones by this time was a major figure in Houston banking. He was chairman of the National Bank of Commerce into which had been merged

80

the institutions previously known as Peoples' State Bank, Labor State Bank, Marine State Bank, and Marine Banking and Trust Company. Jesse Jones decided the healthier banks had to save Houston National and Public National. He called the city's major bankers and business leaders to a meeting in his office in the Gulf Building on Sunday, October 25. The meeting continued off and on through Monday and Monday night. There was agreement that failure of the two shaky banks could cause a panic that might endanger other banks and weaken the public's perception of Houston as the Bright Spot of the Nation. The conferees agreed on a plan to prop up and reorganize Houston National and merge Public National into National Bank of Commerce. (The National Bank of Commerce merged with Texas National in 1964 to become Texas Commerce Bank.)

Jesse Jones' success in the bank rescue probably was one reason President Herbert Hoover named Jones to the Reconstruction Finance Corporation in 1932. President Franklin D. Roosevelt made Jones chairman of the RFC. Jones was trusted by people who did not trust Roosevelt. He was the bridge between the New Deal Administration and the nation's business community. He saved many factories, banks, and some railroads

45

SAM HOUSTON HIGH SCHOOL

46) Sam Houston High School now occupies a building on Irvington, built in the 1950s. The school was in the building pictured here when Johnson was teaching. This building was turned into an administration building for the district in the 1950s and then demolished when the new administration building was built on Richmond Avenue. This is the block bound by Capitol, Austin, Rusk, and Caroline. The privately operated Houston Academy opened on this site in 1859. The public school system acquired the block in 1880 and built the Houston High School here in 1895. Houston High School was renamed Central High before it burned in 1921. This building replaced that one and the school continued to be called Central High until the name was changed to Sam Houston High in 1926. Courtesy Sam Houston High School.

47) Lyndon Johnson lived in a rented room in this house on Hawthorne when he was teaching at Sam Houston High.

48) Movies were the most popular form of entertainment in the 1930s and the main action was downtown. There were three first-run movie palaces on Main Street. Loew's State and the Metropolitan were side by side, in the 100 block. San Jacinto Museum of History, Cecil Thompson Collection, courtesy Houston Library.

from ruin with his handling of the emergency loan program. Jones was head of the RFC until 1939. He was secretary of commerce and federal loan administrator from then until 1945 when he fell out with the Democrats and returned to Houston.

J. W. Sartwelle and a little band of civic leaders organized the Houston Fat Stock Show and Rodeo in 1931 and staged the first show from February 17 to March 3, 1932, in the hall built for the 1928 Democratic Convention. The show moved to the Sam Houston Coliseum in 1938.

Mayor Oscar Holcombe ended the practice of having aldermen heading the city departments. It was a step toward making department heads responsible directly to him. The wrangling over this helped to bring on

48

49

a brief experiment with the city manager form of government during World War II.

George R. Brown was gaining influence in Houston affairs in the early 1930s. He came to Houston in 1926 to open a branch of the construction company his brother Herman and Dan Root had started in Central Texas in 1919. George Brown was the company's front man and strategist. He made friends with the city's most powerful bankers and financiers and for 50 years maintained a hotel suite where these movers and shakers could meet to drink and talk after office hours. The suite was in the

50

49) A showman named Doug Prince ran the biggest hamburger business in town in the 1930s and on through the 50s. This was Prince's Drive-In on Main at Gray, featuring hamburgers at 10 cents each. Courtesy Prince Family.

50) Before he became a famous wild-catter, the late Glenn McCarthy in the 1930s owned and operated two Sinclair service stations. The one at Main and McGowen was demolished. The one at Westheimer and Waugh still stands, disguised as a coffee shop.

51) Only a couple of street names survive from the brief period in the 1930s when Houston had a horse track and legal betting. There is a street named Epsom and a street named Downs but no trace of the stadium or the stables where Epsom Downs was (near the junction of U.S. 59 North and Jensen Drive on the near northeast side).

51

Lamar Hotel, so it was easy for Jesse Jones to drop in. This little group exerted a large influence on politics and civic affairs and Brown and Root became the biggest construction company in the country.

Rain poured down on Harris County in 1935 and produced the worst flood Houston had experienced. Two-thirds of the county was under water. Several blocks of the downtown business district flooded. This flood produced the political pressure that caused congress to approve the Addicks and Barker reservoirs to control the flow of rainwater in the Buffalo Bayou watershed.

KXYZ Radio began broadcasting in 1935 from studios in the Gulf Building. Tilford Jones was the owner.

The Houston Independent School District established in 1935 the junior college that would become the University of Houston. The first classes were held in temporary buildings on the campus of San Jacinto High School. The university moved to the present site on Cullen after Ben Taub and Julius Settegast donated land there in 1939.

Rice graduate Albert Thomas was elected to Congress in 1936. He represented Houston and Harris County there until he died in 1966.

52) Construction of the San Jacinto Monument began during the celebration of the 100th anniversary of the Battle of San Jacinto in 1936. It was designed by Alfred Finn. The federal government put up most of the money. Houston Library.

53) *Albert Thomas came to Houston from Nacogdoches to attend the university then called Rice Institute. He was working as an assistant district attorney in Houston when he decided to run for congress. He was elected and then reelected every two years thereafter until he died. Houston Library.*

53

The city built the golf course in Memorial Park in 1936 with some help from the WPA. The course opened on July 12.

The first air-conditioned, streamlined, stainless steel passenger train arrived in 1936. It was Burlington's Sam Houston Zephyr and it began daily runs between Houston and Dallas-Fort Worth on October 1. Burlington added a second streamliner called the Texas Rocket in 1937. These trains hit between 90 and 100 miles an hour and covered the distance between Houston and Dallas in four hours. Braniff had started air service to Houston in 1935. Eastern started in 1936.

The city in 1937 bought the ten-year-old private airport on Telephone Road that had been known as Carter Field. It became Houston Municipal Airport.

Howard Hughes won the International Harmon Trophy in 1938 by flying around the world in three days, 19 hours, and 14 minutes. He was invited to Houston to be honored with a parade. Hughes flew his plane in from Chicago. He was supposed to land at 11 a.m., July 30, but he got a favorable wind that put him ahead of schedule. The radio stations were set up for live coverage but if the hero arrived before 11 a.m., they would have to interrupt soap operas. One of the station managers got on the tower radio to try to persuade the guest of honor to delay his arrival. But other people's schedules never were very important to Howard Hughes. He just flew on in early. The Houston City Council got carried away and voted to name the airport for Hughes. The decision was rescinded when the city fathers discovered it was not legal to name city properties for people still living.

M. D. Anderson of Anderson Clayton died in 1939 shortly after establishing a foundation to benefit the public, advance knowledge, and alleviate human suffering. It was left to Anderson's trustees, John Freeman, W. B. Bates, and Horace Wilkins to decide what to do with the $20 million Anderson left in the foundation. The trustees were considering a hospital when they learned in 1941 that the legislature had authorized the University of Texas to start a cancer research hospital. The Anderson trustees offered a free site and some help with building costs. The University agreed to put the hospital in Houston and name it for M. D. Anderson. The hospital opened in 1942 in temporary quarters furnished by the Anderson Foundation. Dr. E. W. Bertner was hired as interim director. John Freeman said it was Dr. Berner who first suggested the idea of a medical center.

The late 1930s brought a flurry of public works projects backed by federal money. The Sam Houston Coliseum and Music Hall were completed in 1937 on the site of the 1928 Convention Hall. The monument at the San Jacinto Battleground was completed in 1938. The new Houston City Hall was completed in 1939.

The DePelchin Faith Home for children moved from 2700 Albany to a new campus on North Shepherd at Buffalo Bayou in 1938. Kezia Payne DePelchin had started the home in a cottage on Washington Avenue in 1892.

The 1940 Census credited Houston with a population of 384,514. That was 100,000 people more than were counted in Dallas that year. The population of the county was more than half a million. The popu-

54

54) The Burlington railroad started running diesel streamliners between Houston and Dallas/Fort Worth in the 1930s and discontinued them 30 years later for lack of passengers. Courtesy Edward Bourdon.

55) The school that became the University of Houston was etablished as a junior college in 1935. It moved to the present campus in 1939. This is the atrium in the student center.

56) The University of Houston was added to the state university system in 1963. One of the school's unique features is the School of Hotel and Restaurant Management, endowed by the late hotelman Conrad Hilton.

55

56

57

57) The first airline to fly passengers in and out of Houston was Braniff of Dallas, using what is now Hobby Airport. The year was 1935. Houston Library.

58) There was a big celebration at the airport then called Houston Municipal in 1938. Howard Hughes, Jr., had just set a new record time for flying around the world. He was already living in California full-time but local friends persuaded him to fly in for a celebration in his honor. Houston Library.

59) All three Houston radio stations put the airport welcoming ceremony on the air live. Houston Library.

60) Main Street was festooned with bunting and ticker tape for the Hughes parade and nobody there could have dreamed that the smiling young hero would die of self-neglect on another flight to Houston in 1976. Houston Library.

lation of the state topped six million. The transit system retired its last trolley car in 1940. Work started in 1941 on a new master street plan emphasizing thoroughfares and a loop system. The city and the federal government created in 1941 the low-rent public housing project originally called San Felipe Courts and later renamed Allen Parkway Village. The old Ellington Field was reactivated in 1940 to train bomber pilots, navigators, and bombardiers for the Army Air Corps. The army also

58

59

60

61

62

built a new training base for anti-aircraft units near Hitchcock and named it Camp Wallace, for Colonel Elmer Wallace. He was an artillery officer killed in France in World War I.

Houstonians were shocked the morning of December 7, 1941, by the news of the Japanese attack on Pearl Harbor. Police Chief Ray Ashworth sent a detail of officers under Sergeant Ham Ellisor to guard the Japanese Consulate in the 3400 block of Burlington. Mayor Neal Pickett announced plans on December 12 for recruiting 1,000 air raid wardens.

Camp Wallace was transferred to the navy before the end of the war and the navy closed it in 1946. The navy also had a blimp base near

61) The house where Howard Hughes, Jr. grew up is now part of the campus of the University of St. Thomas. It is on Yoakum. The vault where the Hugheses kept their liquor during Prohibition is still in the basement.

62) Houston Chronicle publisher and financier Jesse Jones, right, became one of the most powerful people in the country during the administration of President Franklin D. Roosevelt, left. Jones was Roosevelt's secretary of commerce and also director of the Reconstruction Finance Corporation. Courtesy Houston Chronicle.

63) The present Houston City Hall was added to the National Register of Historic Places in 1991. It was built by the WPA in 1939. The park between the City Hall and Smith Street had been donated to the city earlier by George Hermann. He wanted to make sure Houston would always have a place where people could sit down or take a nap if they felt like it. The Hermann family's homestead was on this site.

63

Hitchcock. Navy blimp patrols failed to prevent German submarines from sinking tankers in the Gulf. The submarines were the reason the government built the Big Inch and Little Inch pipelines to carry liquid petroleum products from here to the Eastern seaboard. Texas Eastern Transmission Company bought the Big Inch and Little Inch pipelines after the war and converted them to carry natural gas as the Tennessee Gas Transmission Company's pipeline already was doing. Texas oil fields were producing such a surplus of natural gas that many operators were simply flaring it at the wells. The highway between Houston and Galveston was illuminated at night by flares in the oil fields along the way.

The war reduced the number of ships doing business at the Port of Houston and likewise at the Port of Galveston, but the big increase in demand for gasoline brought about expansion of the refineries along the Houston Ship Channel. New plants were built to make synthetic rubber. The army took a big tract of channelside property for an ordnance depot and built the Dickson Gun Plant on the north shore of the channel to make gun barrels. Hughes Tool Company managed the gun plant until it closed in 1945. Two shipyards on the channel turned out small vessels for the navy. Sheffield Steel built in 1942 the ship channel steel plant that was known as Armco when it closed in 1983.

The Japanese sank the cruiser *Houston* in 1942. Houstonians decided they should take responsibility for replacing it. A thousand volunteers

64

64) The Houston Housing Authority tore down blocks of festering slums and the city's fanciest brothel in 1941 to build the low-rent housing project originally named San Felipe Courts. The project is now called Allen Parkway Village and the site it occupies has become very valuable.

65) Cotton broker M. D. Anderson left his fortune when he died in 1939 to be used for the benefit of the public to advance knowledge and alleviate human suffering. Houston Library.

65

66) Anderson's trustees proposed to the University of Texas that a cancer research hospital the legislature had authorized in 1941 should be built in Houston and named for M. D. Anderson. They offered a free site and some help with the building costs. The M. D. Anderson Hospital opened in a temporary location in 1942. The first unit of the present M. D. Anderson opened in 1954 in the Medical Center also created by the Anderson trustees.

66

were sworn into the navy at a ceremony on Main Street to replace the crew. Houstonians bought $85 million worth of war bonds and the navy gave the city's name to a new cruiser already under construction. It became USS *Houston II.*

Voters approved a change in the form of city government in 1942. Administrative responsibility was concentrated in a new office of city manager. There were eight city council members and a mayor. Otis

95

67

68

67) The Baylor College of Medicine was so pleased to get an invitation to move from Dallas to Houston in 1943 that the school made the move before a building could be built. Baylor students attended classes during the first four years the school was in Houston in this warehouse building on what is now Allen Parkway.

68) The first unit of Baylor College of Medicine was the first building completed in the Texas Medical Center. It opened in 1947. The Anderson trustees made the medical school the same offer they had made to the University of Texas: a free site and some help with the building costs. This became the formula for development of the Medical Center.

69) The home the late Mayor Oscar Holcombe built on the boulevard the city later named for him has been donated to the Texas Medical Center by the Holcombe family. It will be a hospice.

69

97

70) Many Houston factories shifted to
production of war materials during World
War II and some new plants were built.
The Brown brothers of Brown and Root
established Brown Shipbuilding Company
at Green's Bayou to build small warships for the navy. Courtesy of Brown
and Root.

Massey was elected mayor. He was the presiding officer of the council.
He attended ceremonies and cut ribbons but he did not run the goverment
the way Houston mayors had before. The new plan was borrowed from
Dallas and former Dallas city manager John North Edy was hired as city
manager.

Plans were completed in 1945 for the Gulf Freeway between Houston
and Galveston and the work began the following year.

The M. D. Anderson Foundation trustees put the keystone in their
medical center plan during World War II. They made an offer of free
land and help with building costs to the Baylor University College of
Medicine. The school moved from Dallas in 1943 and conducted classes
in temporary quarters furnished by the foundation until 1947 when the

first Baylor building in the medical center was completed. The medical school had started in 1900 as the University of Dallas Medical Department. Baylor University took it over in 1903. The university and the medical college have been separate entities since 1969.

The Anderson trustees had decided by 1943 that the medical center should be south of Hermann Park adjacent to Hermann Hospital. Most of the site was owned by the city. It had been bought from the Hermann Estate with the idea that it would be added to Hermann Park. Some prominent citizens objected to having the land used for anything but a park. So the city held an election. The voters approved of selling the land. The Anderson Foundation bought it in 1944 and chartered the Texas Medical Center, Inc., in 1945. The same year the center granted a site and some help with building costs to the proposed St. Luke's Episcopal Hospital and the pattern for development of the medical center was set. St. Luke's opened in 1954, the same year the first permanent unit of the M. D. Anderson Hospital for Cancer Research was completed. Dr. R. Lee Clark had succeeded Dr. Bertner as director of Anderson in 1946. Dr. Bertner went on to be the first president of the Texas Medical Center from 1945 to 1950.

The Houston Chamber of Commerce raised $1 million in 1946 to help pay for the initial work on the University of Texas institutions in the medical center and building has been going on almost continuously ever since.

PART THREE

Development
Since
World War II

"I prophesy that, within 50 years, Texas will lead all other states of the Union in population and wealth, that it will have the most economic and political power of any state and that Houston will be the fourth or fifth city in the United States in point of size."

General Robert E. Wood, Chairman, Sears, 1951.

1) *There was a new star in the Houston firmament in the expansive years following the end of World War II. Glenn H. McCarthy had started drilling oil wells for others in the 1930s. His McCarthy Oil and Gas Corporation had made him rich by 1946 and his lifestyle conformed to the public's conception of the typical Texas oilman. Courtesy Edward Bourdon.*

1

Everything built in Houston before World War II is dwarfed and overshadowed by what has been built since. The dominant buildings on the skyline have been built in the last 20 years. Building permits issued in the five years preceding World War II totalled $100 million. Permits for the year 1948 totalled $271 million. Some of the buildings built then have been torn down to make way for bigger buildings.

Houston annexed another 142 square miles in 1948. This gave the city a total area of 216 square miles and an estimated population of 620,000. The city took in another 104 square miles in 1956 to make a total area of 320 square miles.

Houston had 33 passenger trains arriving and leaving every day in 1945. There were just 30 scheduled airplanes arriving and leaving each day. Work began on the Gulf Freeway under the supervision of James C. Dingwall.

The county contracted for the tunnels under the ship channel in 1947. The Baytown Tunnel and the Washburn Tunnel at Pasadena both were completed in the early 1950s. The Washburn Tunnel was named for longtime Harris County Auditor Harry Washburn.

The navy built a big hospital on Holcombe Boulevard in 1946 and later turned it over to the Veterans' Administration.

The Basilian Fathers established the University of St. Thomas in 1947 in an old mansion on Montrose that originally was the home of developer J. W. Link.

A small group of theater enthusiasts started the Alley Theater in a rented building on South Main in 1947. Nina Vance was the director. Hugh Roy Cullen and his wife Lillie established their Cullen Foundation in 1947 and transferred to it assets worth an estimated $160 million to be used to help educational, medical, and charitable institutions in Texas. Cullen said they didn't want to wait until they were dead to give their money away because they enjoyed the giving of it. He enjoyed the attention their gifts brought him, too. He always made a speech.

Several new petrochemical plants were built on the ship channel during World War II. This trend continued during the years immediately after the war. Blue chip companies invested hundreds of millions of dollars in new plants to extract chemicals from the oil and gas being delivered to the channel area by dozens of pipelines. The channel was deepened to 36 feet.

The Federated department store chain bought the venerable Foley Brothers Dry Goods Company in 1945 and started planning a big new building on Main between Lamar and Dallas.

Former mayor Oscar Holcombe ran for the office again in 1946 promising to do away with the city manager arrangement. Houstonians elected

Holcombe and then approved the charter changes he designed. Holcombe combined the powers of the city manager and the mayor in the mayor's office and the system he designed hasn't been changed since. No mayor in America has more power than the mayor of Houston.

George and Herman Brown built small warships for the navy during the war at a shipyard on the channel at Green's Bayou. They used that site following the end of the war to begin pioneering the design and construction of offshore oil rigs. The Browns and others formed the Texas Eastern Company in 1947.

The golf cart was born in Houston in 1946. Dodge dealer Dick Jackson was determined to go on playing golf after his arthritis prevented him from doing the walking required. Jackson had his shop convert a 3-wheel Cushman scooter to transport him and his clubs around the Houston Country Club course.

The Houston Horse Show Association was chartered in 1946 to put on shows to raise money for a childrens' hospital. The shows were staged at J. S. Abercrombie's Pin Oak Stables on Post Oak Road until 1975. The Texas Childrens' Foundation was chartered in 1947 by Leopold Meyer, George Butler, Raymond Cohen, Nina Cullinan, H. J. Ehlers, John K. Glen, David Greer, Martha Lovett, A. L. Mitchell, and George Salmon. The Texas Medical Center set aside a site in 1948 and Texas Children's Hospital opened in 1953, with J. S. Abercrombie personally underwriting some of the expense.

2

3

2) McCarthy decided to celebrate his Irish heritage by building a hotel and calling it the Shamrock. He got actor Pat O'Brien to come to Houston for the groundbreaking in 1946 at the site he chose on South Main. Courtesy Houston Chronicle.

3) O'Brien came back in 1949 for the Shamrock grand opening, on St. Patrick's Day. McCarthy had masses of shamrocks

flown in from Ireland for the occasion. Photo courtesy Ed Bourdon.

4) The Basilian Fathers established the University of St. Thomas on Montrose Boulevard in 1947, with administrative offices in the home Montrose Addition developer J. W. Link built for himself. This mansion was later the home of oil millionaire T. P. Lee.

4

5

5) Nina Vance was named director when the Alley Theater was organized in Houston in 1947. She guided the theater until she died in 1980. Courtesy Edward Bourdon.

6) The Alley Theater took its name from the original location in the building at the end of this little alley off South Main Street. The theater operated for several years in an old fan factory off Smith Street after it moved out of this location at the suggestion of the fire marshall.

7) The new Foley's department store opened in 1947 in a building covering the entire block bound by Main, Dallas, Travis, and Lamar. Foley's had been bought a little earlier by the Federated chain. The original name had been Foley Brothers and the former Foley Brothers building in the 400 block of Main became the home of the first Joske's store in Houston when Foley's moved to this location. Courtesy Edward Bourdon.

6

Joske's of San Antonio opened a Houston branch in 1948 in the Main Street Building Foley's had just vacated. The original Houston Joske's sold only home furnishings.

The Baylor College of Medicine named Dr. Michael DeBakey chairman of its department of surgery in 1948. This pioneering cardiovascular surgeon made Baylor and Methodist Hospital world famous. DeBakey was born in Lake Charles, LA, and trained at Tulane. He served as president of the medical school from 1969 through 1979.

There were some clubs in Houston and Harris County in the 1940s where gambling was carried on fairly openly. Slot machines and bookies were prevalent. Jakie Freedman's big white showplace on South Main was especially blatant. Freedman offered dining and dancing, drinking, craps, and roulette for the carriage trade. No riffraff and no strangers got past the guardhouse at the entrance to his grounds. Freedman moved on to Las Vegas after Buster Kern was elected sheriff in 1948. Kern put the lid on the town and some former lawmen spent the next several years explaining their tax returns to the IRS. Kern served until 1972 when he was defeated by Jack Heard. He died in 1981.

It was still unusual in 1949 for something happening in Houston to attract national attention, but the opening of the Shamrock Hotel on the night of March 17 of that year got plenty of attention. Builder Glenn McCarthy made sure of it by importing 175 Hollywood personalities for the party and arranging for Dorothy Lamour's NBC radio show to originate in the new hotel's glittering Emerald Room. A lot of people crashed the party. They caused so much noise and commotion that NBC cut the Lamour show off the air. The microphones picked up some language before the show was cut off that had never been heard on network radio before; expletives in fairly common use but not then permitted on the airwaves. It is generally believed that Edna Ferber found

8

8) The legislature established Texas
State University for Negroes in Houston
in 1947 and this was the school that
became Texas Southern University. The
campus is on Wheeler Street within a
few blocks of the University
of Houston main campus.

9) The city's first television station began
operations in 1949 in this Quonset hut off
South Post Oak. The station was here
only five years and the building was used
as a hay barn until it was demolished in
1990. The first station was Channel 2,
originally called KLEE-TV, later KPRC-
TV.

10) Marvin Zindler did some of the first
TV news reports in Houston, free-lancing
for KLEE-TV and KPRC-TV. Courtesy
Channel 13.

9

some of the inspiration for her novel Giant in Glenn McCarthy and the opening of the Shamrock.

Television came to Houston on January 1, 1949, when hotel man Albert Lee put KLEE-TV on the air on Channel 2. The station did not prosper and Lee was ready to sell it a couple of years later. The Houston Post Company bought it. The Post company already owned KPRC radio and so changed the name of the TV station to KPRC-TV. It was the only TV station in town for several years. Channel 11 started in Galveston as KGUL-TV in 1953 and moved to Houston in 1958. That's when the call letters were changed to KHOU-TV. Paul Taft and associates put Channel 11 on the air. They sold it to the Corinthian chain and that chain was absorbed into Dun and Bradstreet and then sold to A. H. Belo Company in 1984. KTRK-TV, Channel 13, went on the air in 1954. It was owned originally by a syndicate of wealthy Houstonians including Roy Hofheinz and Jesse Jones' nephew, John T. Jones. They sold it in 1967 to the Capital Cities chain.

The Census of 1950 made Houston the 14th biggest city in the country with a population of 596,163. There was a big boom in air-conditioning between 1945 and 1950 and Houston became known as the most air-conditioned city in the world. Some observers have claimed that Houston never could have become an important city were it not for air-conditioning. Probably somebody in Houston would have invented air-conditioning if somebody else had not. George Brown would have seen to it. He saw to it that Rice got a new football stadium when it needed one in 1950. Brown and Root built it in 9 months, charged the school only the cost, and had the 70,000-seat stadium completed in time for the first game of the 1950 season. Sixty-eight thousand fans saw Rice beat Santa Clara 27-7 in that game on September 30.

Senator Joe McCarthy and his anti-Communist campaign had substantial support in Houston in the early 1950s. The senator drew a large

11

12

11) *The earliest picture of the author on television is this shot a viewer snapped off her TV screen. Foley's had just the one store downtown at the time. The company was one of the earliest regular sponsors of TV news.*

12) *The first full-time television news cameraman in Houston was Bob Gray at Channel 2. Courtesy Bob Gray.*

13) *The city's first television news director was Pat Flaherty of Channel 2, in the wagon, on the right. Pat was one of the founders of the Salt Grass Trail Ride in 1952. This is the granddaddy of the trail rides preceding the stock show and rodeo.*

13

crowd when he came to town to speak in the Sam Houston Coliseum on September 18, 1950. Hugh Roy Cullen introduced him. Some Houston women formed their own Communist fighting organization. The Minute Women got one of their members, Dallas Dyer, elected to the board of the Houston Independent School District in 1952, and exerted considerable influence over board policies for a few years.

Methodist Hospital moved to the Texas Medical Center in 1951, and in 1952 the phenomenon known as the Salt Grass Trail Ride was born. The birthplace was the Cork Club in the Shamrock Hotel. A few of the directors of the Houston Fat Stock Show were having drinks with rodeo producer Reese Lockett, the show's advertising agent Charlie Geizendanner, and Channel 2 general manager Jack Harris. Lockett was complaining about having been stranded on some airline flight by bad weather and he said he would not again go any place he could not get back to his home in Brenham from on horseback. Somebody said then he couldn't come to Houston and Lockett said he had ridden from Brenham to Houston many times, in the old days, driving cows to the salt grass on the coast in the wintertime. Somebody dared him to prove it by doing it again. Geizendanner recognized this as a possible promotion for the stock show. Harris said if Lockett made the ride, Channel 2 news director Pat Flaherty would travel with him.

Geizendanner's assistant, Maudeen Marks, persuaded her rancher father Emil Marks to furnish an antique wagon and a team of mules. Flaherty rode in the wagon, and Marks' foreman John Warnash drove the mules. Lockett and Marks rode horses. The ride ended at the Channel 2 studios before live cameras. Some viewers thought it looked like fun. People began lining up to make the next ride. As a promotional stunt, it was a great success. The number of trail rides and trail riders has been growing ever since.

111

Polio took its greatest toll in Houston in 1953. There were 125 paralytic cases that year. It would be two more years before Jonas Salk would perfect his vaccine. Dr. Walter Quebedeaux was appointed in 1953 to the new position of director of pollution control for Harris County. He did some pioneering and ruffled some feathers but he was still on the job when he died of a heart attack in 1976.

Houston got the first educational television station in the country in 1953. KUHT-TV was licensed to the University of Houston and the Houston Independent School District.

More corporations were moving their headquarters to Houston. Continental Oil established headquarters here in 1950. Prudential Insurance established regional headquarters in a big new building on Holcombe Boulevard the same year. Mobil, Gulf, Texaco, Tidewater Associated, and Sunray Mid-Continent all expanded their Houston headquarters during the 1950s. The Ethyl Corporation opened a new $50 million plant on the ship channel in 1952.

The city was relying entirely upon underground water. But the water table was dropping and the land was subsiding, and it was increasingly plain that another source of water had to be found. Work started on Lake Houston on the San Jacinto in 1952. The lake was completed in 1954 and the city began to deliver surface water to customers in the ship channel area.

Voters in 1952 rejected a proposal for a bond issue to finance a new and bigger airport, so the city began some improvements to the Municipal Airport, including a new terminal building.

Oscar Holcombe had been reelected twice since he was returned to the mayor's office in 1946 and he was planning to run again in 1952

14) KUHT-TV, operated by the University of Houston, is the oldest educational television station in the United States. The station went on the air on Channel 8 in 1953. It now operates in the building built for KNUZ-TV. This building on Cullen was also occupied by Channel 13 from 1954 until 1962.

15) Paul Taft and his partners in KGUL-TV, Channel 11, got permission from the Federal Communications Commission in 1958 to move that CBS affiliate to Houston. The owners changed the name to KHOU-TV and built the studios the station still occupies on Allen Parkway. KGUL-TV had started operations in Galveston in 1953.

16) Channel 13, KTRK-TV, is the ABC affiliate in Houston. The station moved to its present location on Bissonnet in 1962. Channel 13 began operations in 1954 in the former KNUZ-TV studios on Cullen.

14

15

16

17) *The original Houston television station moved from the Quonset hut to a new studio on South Post Oak in 1954 and then to this studio on the Southwest Freeway in Sharpstown in 1972.*

17

when his support dried up. He had usually enjoyed the backing of the Main Street establishment, consisting mostly of the rich and powerful men in the habit of meeting in George Brown's suite at the Lamar Hotel. They and Holcombe understood each other well. But in 1952 the men in Suite 8-F thought Holcombe stood a good chance of losing. The other major candidates were Councilman Louie Welch and former county judge Roy Hofheinz. The establishment preferred Hofheinz. He and Holcombe were so advised. Holcombe got out of the race and Hofheinz was elected.

Hofheinz had a brilliant mind and a forceful personality. He set out to remake Houston. He wanted more public works and more taxes to pay for them and he was soon in a hopeless deadlock with the more conservative city council. Council meetings were often interrupted by shouting and name calling. But Hofheinz was elected to another term in 1954. He and the council continued to disagree on the budget and nearly everything else. The council drew up 18 proposed amendments to the city charter to reduce the power of the mayor. Hofheinz forced another proposal onto the ballot. His amendment would move the city election date up one year. He made it plain that he hoped to get a new council elected.

114

18) Walter Quebedeaux was a pioneer in the campaign against pollution of the air and water in this part of the world. The Harris County Commissioners Court named him County Pollution Control Director in 1953 and he worked at that job until he died in 1976. The commissioners hailed him as an inspiration to those who followed him in the field. Courtesy Mrs. Walter Quebedeaux.

18

19) The Houston Chamber of Commerce made a fuss over Barney McCasland when he moved to Houston in 1954. The chamber calculated that the population of Greater Houston reached an even one million when McCasland moved here. He was awarded some prizes and sent on a flying trip around the country to notify other cities of the Houston milestone. McCasland was later transferred to Midland. Courtesy Houston Magazine.

19

The council drew up a set of impeachment charges and started holding hearings. Establishment lawyer Jack Binion stepped into Hofheinz's corner and outfoxed the council at every turn. Hofheinz was still in office on election day. The voters turned down all the amendments proposed by the council and approved only the Hofheinz proposal for a new election. A few people tried to tell Hofheinz that some of the voters might be anxious for a chance to vote for a new mayor, but he said the people

115

wanted him and a new city council. He named a committee to pick a slate of council candidates and then went off on a trip to Europe. Hofheinz found when he returned that Oscar Holcombe was getting ready to run for mayor again. He didn't need anyone to explain to him that Holcombe had the support of the establishment. Holcombe wouldn't be running without it.

Hofheinz started a slashing attack on Holcombe and Jesse Jones and the Suite 8-F crowd. He said the voters had to choose between him and the "fat cats." He made some of the most abrasive campaign speeches ever made on Houston television. The medium was still new. Very few politicians had learned how to use it. Holcombe never did learn. Hofheinz told people the television camera was the greatest lie detector ever invented. He said no one could get away with lying to the camera. It was another way of saying that whatever he said on television must be true and he soon made it plain there was hardly anything he would not say on television. The voters learned more from Hofheinz's speeches that season than they had ever known before about who the main men in the establishment were — and they sided with the establishment. Six of the incumbent councilmen were reelected and Oscar Holcombe was elected mayor. Former councilman Louie Welch was returned to the council to continue his campaign for mayor. One of Hofheinz's former supporters in 8-F said, "Roy just got too big for his britches." Hofheinz departed from the city hall in a new Cadillac limousine he bought especially for the occasion.

A number of public works projects were carried out during the stormy three years of the Hofheinz administration. The Music Hall and Coliseum were remodelled. Work was started on the extension of Memorial Drive from Shepherd into the city and on the Elysian Overpass. New restrictions were imposed on parking on downtown streets. Most of the streets down-

20) A few preservationists organized the Harris County Heritage Society in 1954 to save this old house. It was built in 1847 by Nathaniel Kellum on what was then the western edge of town. The city bought the house and the land around it in the 1890s for what became Sam Houston Park. The house was park headquarters for a time and then it was used as a warehouse. There was a fire in 1954 and the city was on the verge of demolishing what was left when the preservationists stepped in and persuaded City Council to let them restore the building. The restoration was completed in 1958 and the Heritage Society has since moved several other historic buildings to the park. This one is on its original site.

21) The old City Hall building was badly damaged by fire in 1960 and then torn down. Part of the building was being used as a bus station when the fire occurred. This is the downtown block the Allen brothers originally called Congress Square because they hoped it would be the site of the capitol of the republic. It has been called Market Square since the first city hall was built here because the city hall was also the city market. The market had outgrown the square by the time the city government moved from this building to the

21

present City Hall in 1939. The city built a market for farmers and produce merchants nearby and it operated until the 1950s. Houston Library.

22) Some farmers bring their produce now to the Farmers' Cooperative Market on Airline Drive and many thrifty homemakers shop here. The big dealers do business at Produce Row off Old Spanish Trail.

22

23

25

24

town were converted to one-way, and planning of the major thoroughfare system began. The new airport terminal was completed and when it opened in 1954, the name of the airport was changed to Houston International.

The Gulf Freeway reached Galveston in 1953. It was one of the most advanced highways of its time but the state highway engineers have been adding lanes and overpasses almost continuously ever since.

Developer Frank Sharp was finishing up the Oak Forest subdivision when he announced plans in 1954 for a much bigger development southwest of the city. He projected 25,000 homes and an investment of $400 million in the Sharpstown development. Most of the land involved had previously been held by Glenn McCarthy. He had hoped to prevail upon the city to put the new airport there. He had planned other developments around the Shamrock Hotel and wanted to skew the city's growth in that direction. He gave up on the airport idea when the city's bond proposal failed. McCarthy was in deep financial trouble by this time. The hotel and his oil and gas interests were mortgaged. He couldn't meet the payments of his debts. Equitable Life Assurance took over the Shamrock in 1953.

New suburbs were sprouting all around Houston in the 1950s. The laws in effect in those days allowed cities and the residents of suburbs beyond the city limits to ambush each other. A city council could vote in the middle of the night, with no warning, to annex adjacent territory. The residents of that territory were powerless to prevent the completion of this process and had no choice except to begin paying city taxes. But

23) The area around Market Square is the oldest part of Houston. The oldest surviving commercial building in town faces the square on Congress between Milam and Travis. This building probably was built about 1848. It housed a bakery and a stage station at different, earlier times. It is now a bar.

24) There was a little movement in the 1960s to preserve the old buildings in the Market Square area and a number of them were turned into night clubs and bars but there was not enough business to support them all and some property owners were more interested in redevelopment. The

building pioneer grocer Henry Henke built on Market Square in the 1920s was renovated and modernized in 1982. The original building on this corner at Congress and Milam was Pamelia Mann's Mansion House.

25) The building at 806 Commerce had been a warehouse and the home of several commercial enterprises before a law firm bought it in the late 1970s and turned it into an office building.

26) The first big regional shopping center in Houston was Gulfgate, opening in 1956 on the Gulf Freeway at the projected Loop 610 interchange.

27) Very little was happening before 1957 along Farm Road 1960 in northwest Harris County. Most people called it Jack Rabbit Road and it was just two lanes wide. Then Jackie Burke and Jimmy Demeret built the Champions Golf Club and people started moving to FM 1960. It has been one of the fastest growing areas in Harris County ever since.

26

they could save themselves from annexation if they moved first, by calling an election on incorporation. Residents of the suburbs along Memorial Drive heard in December of 1954 that the city was about to annex them. There was a flurry of sudden incorporation elections resulting in the west side villages now surrounded by Houston. The city and some of the other established municipalities in Harris County sometimes surprised each other with midnight annexations to preserve tax bases and prevent encirclement. At one time in 1960, Houston annexed all the unincorporated area in the county temporarily, as a means of settling a territorial dispute with Pasadena. This disorderly state of affairs brought on a new state law in 1963, taking the element of surprise out of annexations and incorporations. Houston City Councilman Louie Welch engineered this change as president of the Texas Municipal League.

Battlestein's Main Street clothing store opened a branch on South Shepherd in 1954, beginning the retailers' march to the suburbs. Battlestein's started as a tailor shop in the 300 block of Fannin in 1897. The founder was Philip Battlestein.

The Houston Country Club bought a new site on Woodway in 1954 and completed a new clubhouse and golf course there in 1957. A group headed by Gus Wortham acquired the old course on South Wayside, operated it for a while, and then sold it to the city in 1974.

Houston was about as rigidly segregated as any city in the South at the end of World War II. The pattern of segregation had developed gradually over the years after the end of Reconstruction. The legislature adopted the poll tax and the politicians devised a system of white primaries to discourage blacks from voting. Many freed slaves had moved from the country into the cities after Emancipation because of false rumors that the Union was going to do something for them. Their descendants crowded into slums near downtown Houston.

Texas and the other states of the old Confederacy adopted a series of "Jim Crow" laws to keep the races separated. Railroads were required to furnish separate compartments and separate waiting rooms for black passengers. Black people could occupy only certain seats on streetcars and buses. School districts were required by the state constitution to maintain separate schools for blacks and whites. All public buildings in Houston had separate restrooms and water fountains for blacks. No restaurant would serve blacks and whites in the same room. Black people were seldom seen in the Main Street stores.

The United States Supreme Court was still following the doctrine that separate schools were all right if they were reasonably equal, when a black postal employee in Houston filed an application for admission to the University of Texas Law School in 1946. Heman Sweatt met all the requirements, but he was rejected because he was black. He filed a federal lawsuit, strongly supported by black publisher Carter Wesley. The state opposed the suit, but quickly established a law school for blacks in Austin and created the Texas State University for Negroes out of what had been the Houston College for Negroes. This school became Texas Southern University in 1951. The Supreme Court decided the separate law schools were not equal and in 1950 ordered the U. T. Law School to admit qualified black students. The court abandoned the separate-but-equal doctrine altogether in 1954 and called for an end to segregated schools.

28

28) The Houston School Board was desegregated before any Houston schools were. Hattie May White was elected to the board in 1958 while the board majority was using every tactic to delay compliance with desegregation orders. Mrs. White served on the board until 1967.

29) George Bush left the oil business behind in 1958 and moved from Midland to Houston to go into politics. He is the first adopted Texan to be elected President of the United States.

30) The home cottonman Will Clayton and his wife Susan had built on Caroline in 1916 was donated in 1958 to the city library. It houses the library's genealogical branch.

29

30

The court banned segregation on interstate trains and buses in 1955. Segregated seating already had ended on Houston buses, in 1954. "Colored" waiting rooms began to disappear.

The lawsuit that forced desegration of the Houston public schools was filed in federal court in 1956. Two black students named Delores Ross and Beneva Williams asked to be admitted to the white schools near their homes. The court told the school district to begin desegregating. The voters elected a black woman to the school board in 1958 but no classes were integrated until 1960 when Federal Judge Ben Connally ordered the district to begin integrating first grade classes. Twelve black students were enrolled that fall in previously all white schools.

Desegregation proceeded at the rate of one grade a year and in 1965 the school board proposed a $60 billion bond issue to pay for new school buildings. Black leaders said the plan was to locate the new schools in areas where one race or the other was dominant, so that integration would be minimized when all the grades finally were desegregated. Rev. Bill Lawson of the Wheeler Avenue Baptist Church organized a campaign against the bond issue, with the support of young Barbara Jordan and young Mickey Leland, among others. Voters approved the board's proposal by a margin of more than two to one. It didn't mean the voters thought Lawson and company were mistaken about the purpose. The remaining grades were desegregated the following year. The movement of white families from the Houston district to suburban school districts was already underway.

Black students began staging sit-in demonstrations in coffee shops and lunchrooms in 1960 to force an end to segregation there. The first place they visited was the lunch counter in the Weingarten supermarket on Almeda, near the edge of a black neighborhood. They also visited Woolworth's, Walgreen's, Grant's, and the City Hall cafeteria. They usually were not served. The lunch counters closed, in most cases, and the

123

31) *The new building the Humble Company put up on Bell in 1960 has changed names. The company is now Exxon and this is the Exxon Building. The Petroleum Club occupies the top two floors. There was an observation deck on top when the building was new but it has been closed. A 44-story building is no longer remarkable.*

31

demonstrators were left sitting. The students followed a different plan when they moved the action to Main Street. They worked out in advance an arrangement with Max Levine at Foley's that allowed several black students to be served at the Foley's lunch counter. They were gone before reporters and photographers learned about it and that broke the ice. The City Hall cafeteria began serving blacks. Mayor Lewis Cutrer ordered an end to segregation at the city swimming pools in 1963. Mayor Roy Hofheinz had removed the "White" and "Colored" signs from the city hall in the early 1950s. Hotels quietly began admitting black guests.

There were a couple of disturbances on the campus of Texas Southern University during the middle 1960s. Several dozen students started throwing things after a pep rally in November, 1965. Police closed off the area, questioned dozens of students and arrested four of them. One officer was wounded. The other disturbance, in May, 1967, left several people injured. One police officer was killed, probably by a ricocheting bullet from another officer's gun. Four students were arrested.

The Houston Chamber of Commerce calculated that the population of the greater Houston area would reach one million in July, 1954. The chamber appointed a committee to decide exactly which newcomer would

124

be number one million. The committee picked a Cities Service transferee named Barney McCasland. He was awarded the title "Mr. Million," given a lot of gifts, and led through a series of public relations exercises. McCasland was later transferred away as oil people often were, then, but others kept coming. The Hilton Hotel chain took over operation of the Shamrock Hotel in 1954 and took title in 1955. A portrait of Conrad Hilton went up in the elevator lobby where Glenn McCarthy's portrait had hung.

A new produce terminal was completed off Old Spanish Trail in 1954 replacing the public market that had sprawled over several downtown city blocks near Market Square where it had started.

Some city officials, and civic and business leaders were still convinced the city would have to have another airport and some were concerned that by the time the voters were convinced, it might be difficult to find a tract of land big enough and close enough to town. The powerful men with keys to Lamar Hotel Suite 8-F never had been taken with Glenn McCarthy's scheme. Their interests were downtown. They didn't want the town skewed to the south. Several of them formed a syndicate they called Jetero Corporation to begin buying up land north of the city. The buyers, of course, didn't tell the sellers what they were doing but they apparently had an understanding with Mayor Holcombe that they would sell the site to the city at the price they paid when the city was ready to move.

There were 475,000 motor vehicles registered in Harris County by 1955 and 8,000 of them were air-conditioned. Neiman-Marcus came to Houston that year. The Dallas company bought out Ben Wolfman's Fashion store in the Kirby Building on Main Street. That store in the Kirby Building was closed when Neiman's moved to the Galleria in 1969.

The Houston Grand Opera was established in 1955. Houston voters in 1956 approved a plan to expand the port and buy the Long Reach

32) Developer Frank Sharp completed the first fully air-conditioned shopping mall in Houston in 1961. His offices and his Sharpstown State Bank were in the dark glass building in the background.

33) *Lawyer Barbara Jordan was often on the podium at black rallies and protest meetings in Houston in the 1960s. She was elected to the Texas Senate in 1966 and served three terms in the U.S. House of Representatives before she retired in 1978 to teach at the Lyndon B. Johnson School of Public Affairs at the University of Texas in Austin. Courtesy Texas Southern University.*

33

34

docks from Anderson Clayton Company. Jesse Jones died in 1956, leaving most of his fortune to a charitable foundation he called Houston Endowment, Incorporated. Jones owned or controlled 49 buildings when he died.

The Second National Bank moved off Main Street in 1956 to a new building on Travis and changed its name to Bank of the Southwest. The bank's building was the biggest in town for a little while.

Gulfgate Shopping Center opened in 1956 with David Daum as manager. Gulfgate was the first big regional shopping center in Houston. It

35

34) *Houstonians staged a parade and barbecue on July 4, 1962, to welcome the astronauts. The National Aeronautics and Space Administration transferred the seven original astronauts here when the agency started building the space center at Clear Lake. Real estate developer Frank Sharp offered the spacemen each a free home in his Sharpstown subdivision. The space agency told them to decline and they all settled in the Clear Lake area. Courtesy* Houston Chronicle.

35) *President John Kennedy came to Texas in the fall of 1963 to try to get the warring factions of the Democratic Party united behind the reelection campaign he was planning. He spent part of the evening of November 21 at a dinner in the Sam Houston Coliseum in honor of Houston Congressman Albert Thomas. The president spoke about the veteran Congressman's vision. He and Vice President Johnson and their party flew on to Fort Worth that night and on to Dallas the morning of November 22. Albert Thomas is on the left in this photograph. The man next to him is Rice President Carey Croneis. Courtesy* Houston Chronicle.

was built around an open mall that was covered over and later air-conditioned.

The Texas Highway Department in the 1950s was studying a realignment of U.S. 59 South, which at the time went out South Main to Missouri City. There was some energetic lobbying by real estate interests, including former Mayor Hofheinz and his partner R. E. Bob Smith. Hofheinz owned 70 acres of land surrounding his home on Yorktown between San Felipe and Westheimer. Hofheinz and Smith had a plan to develop a regional shopping center on this site and they put on all the pressure they could to get the proposed Southwest Freeway routed by this property. But they were outgunned by Frank Sharp. He offered free right of way through Sharpstown and he got many of the other property owners along the route he favored to do the same thing. The highway department decided in 1957 to take the new highway through Sharpstown. Hofheinz and Smith abandoned their shopping center plans. Frank Sharp built Sharpstown Center.

The Royal Dutch Airline, KLM, started flights between Houston and Amsterdam in 1957, the city's first direct air link with Europe.

Oshman's bought the Levy Brothers store at Main and Walker in 1957 and converted it to an Oshman's outlet. Abe and Leo Levy had started

36) The space base caused a building boom at Clear Lake. The Nassau Bay Motor Inn went up directly across the newly-named NASA 1 from the main entrance to the base. The broadcast networks all sent their main news anchors down to cover the first few space flights to be controlled by the base. NBC-TV had Chet Huntley and David Brinkley working in a glass box on the roof of this hotel.

36

37

37) The land the Humble Company donated to Rice University for the space base had earlier been the Jim West ranch. Rice kept that part of the donated site that included the sumptuous West ranch house, refurbished it, and rented it to the Lunar and Planetary Institute. The late Jim West had bought the ranch with money he made in timber and land. Oil was discovered on the property. Humble bought it for the oil and still had several thousand acres left after donating 1,000 acres for the base.

Levy Brothers in 1887 at Main and Congress, but the store was owned by the National Department Store chain when it was sold to Oshman's. Jake Oshman had opened his first sporting goods store in 1932 at Capitol and Fannin.

Harris County established a new park commission in 1958 to look into building a new stadium to accommodate the stock show. Some hoped such a stadium might bring a big league ball club to Houston. Banker Bill Kirkland was chairman of the park board.

The ship channel was deepened to 40 feet in 1958 and Congressman Albert Thomas persuaded the army to give up the San Jacinto Ordnance Depot to make room for more industries on the channel. A new congressional district was created in 1958 including a large part of southern Harris County. County Judge Bob Casey won the election to represent the new 22nd District and the Houston area had two members in the U.S. House of Representatives. Oilman George Bush moved to Houston from Midland in 1958. He announced he was giving up business to devote the rest of his life to public service. He was elected chairman of the Harris County Republican Party in 1963.

Jet passenger liners began flying regularly from Houston International in 1958; and the Harris County Heritage Society completed the restoration of the 1847 Kellum-Noble house in Sam Houston Park.

129

38) The most eye-catching exhibit in the Houston Museum of Natural Science is the skeleton of a diplodocus. Some of the bones are the real thing, found in Wyoming. The others are man-made replicas. The museum is in the northwest corner of Hermann Park. It opened at this location in 1964 but the organization goes back to 1909. J. Griffis Smith, courtesy Houston Museum of Natural Science.

39) Oilman John Mecom spent a fortune turning the old Warwick apartment hotel into a hotel for the rich and famous. Mecom bought the building at auction in 1962 and opened it as the Warwick Hotel in 1964. He also built the fountains in the traffic circle at South Main and Montrose.

39

40

40) *The world's first air-conditioned baseball stadium opened in Houston in 1965 with a flourish. President and Mrs. Johnson came and watched the first game in the stadium that Houston Sports Association President Roy Hofheinz had decided to call the Astrodome. Harris County owns the stadium and the official name is Harris County Domed Stadium. Hofheinz lost control of the sports association that holds the lease, before he died, but the name he chose is the name that stuck. This is not inappropriate. Hofheinz contributed several times as much time, energy, and imagination as any other individual to the campaign that produced the stadium and won the National League baseball franchise for Houston. The man behind Mrs. Johnson in this photograph is Welcome Wilson. The men behind the president are Johnny Goyen and Archie Bennett. The man behind Roy Hofheinz, on the right is Rufus Youngblood of the Secret Service. Courtesy Associated Press.*

The College Committee of the Union Baptist Association bought 390 acres on the proposed Southwest Freeway from Frank Sharp with $760,000, borrowed from Rice University. Houston Baptist College opened there in 1963 with Dr. W. H. Hinton as president. The college became Houston Baptist University in 1975.

41) Kenneth Schnitzer started the Greenway Plaza office and residential development in 1967 on some vacant land he bought at Richmond Avenue and Buffalo Speedway.

41

The Humble Company announced plans in the late 50s for a new headquarters building on Bell. It would be 44 stories. It was the tallest building in the south when it was finished in 1960.

Oilman Bud Adams was shopping for a National Football League franchise in 1959. He didn't find any for sale, but the NFL decided that year to take in two more clubs. Houston could have had one of those new franchises except that the NFL required the franchisee to have access to a stadium seating 50,000 people. The only stadium in Houston that big was the one at Rice, and Rice was not interested in making it available. The new NFL franchises went to Dallas and Minnesota. Clint Murchison got the Dallas franchise for the Cowboys. Lamar Hunt of Dallas had also wanted a franchise. He and Bud Adams pooled their disappointment and started the American Football League. They gave franchises to themselves, Denver, Boston, Los Angeles, and New York. Adams' Houston Oilers played their home games in Jeppeson Stadium on Cullen until 1965.

The 1960 Census made Houston the sixth largest city in the United States with a population of 938,219. The building boom continued in the downtown area. The First City National Bank Building, Cullen

132

42

42) Schnitzer is a native Houstonian. Greenway Plaza is his monument but he also built several major downtown buildings including the Allied Bank Tower and four of the buildings in Allen Center. Schnitzer is one of the two developers most responsible for transforming Houston's appearance. Courtesy Schnitzer Enterprises.

43) The biggest developer in Houston during the boom years of the 60s, 70s, and early 80s was Gerald Hines. He came to Houston from Indiana in 1948, renovated a small office building in 1951, and built several small office buildings on Richmond Avenue before he hit the big time with the Galleria. Courtesy Gerald D. Hines Interests.

43

Center, The Sheraton-Lincoln Building, the World Trade Center, the new Federal building, and the new main Post Office were all under construction. Fourteen major new office buildings were completed in the downtown area between 1960 and 1969. In the same period, Gerald Hines started building the Galleria, Kenneth Schnitzer started Greenway Plaza, and the American General Company built the first building in what would become the American General Center on Allen Parkway at Waugh Drive. Tall buildings were no longer confined to downtown and South Main Street.

Rice Institute changed its name to Rice University in 1960 and, four years later, got a court order permitting it to disregard the provision in William Marsh Rice's will that limited admission to white students.

The city of Houston in 1960 took title to the new airport site the Jetero syndicate had been holding. Ralph Johnston accepted the city's check for $1,980,463. There was official praise for the generosity and farsightedness of the syndicate members. If any of the members had bought on their own account land that would appreciate because of the airport, nobody was inclined to complain about it. It was the Houston way. Work began in 1962 on what became Houston Intercontinental

45

46

44) This is what the intersection of Westheimer and Post Oak looked like from the air in the middle 1950s. There was a country schoolhouse on the site where the Galleria opened in 1970 and a country store on the site now occupied by Dillard's. Courtesy Gerald Hines Interests.

45) It was the Galleria that really set off the Westheimer-Post Oak boom, but Sakowitz had built a big store ten years earlier on the northwest corner of the

intersection. Joske's built the store that is now Dillard's on the southeast corner of the intersection in 1963.

46) Gerald Hines' trademark is striking design. Philip Johnson designed the building Hines built for Pennzoil in 1972. Pennzoil Place is the black glass building on the left in this photograph. The white building on the right is One Shell Plaza, built by Hines for Shell Oil in 1971.

Airport. The name strikes some travelers as pretentious since every other city is satisfied to have an "International" airport. But Houstonians are not embarrassed about having the only intercontinental airport. The former Houston International Airport was renamed for the late former Governor W. P. Hobby when Intercontinental opened in 1969. Governor Hobby had died in 1964 at 86. The old city hall building on Market Square burned in 1960. The city had rented the building out after the new city hall was built in 1939. Part of the old building was being used as a bus terminal when the fire occurred. Some downtown interests pressed the city to sell the site for development, but the city council decided to make it a park.

Will Clayton's wife Susan died in 1960 at the age of 79. Susan Clayton had bought up an old slum area known as Schrimpf Alley in 1951 and donated it to the city for a public housing project called Clayton Homes.

Congressman Albert Thomas learned in 1961 that the National Aeronautics and Space Administration was shopping for a site for a center to control manned spaceflight. Thomas steered the NASA people to Harris County. The Humble Company owned 30,000 acres on the north side of Clear Lake. George Brown was chairman of trustees at Rice University. He and Humble president Morgan Davis arranged a transfer of 1,000 acres of that land to Rice so Rice could offer it, free, to the space agency. There was not a better offer. NASA's James Webb announced in September, 1961, that the Manned Spacecraft Center would be built on the site offered by Rice. Congressman Thomas said the credit was due to President John Kennedy, Vice President Lyndon Johnson, Morgan Davis, and George Brown. George Brown always said Thomas played the key role. Thomas was chairman of the House subcommittee that controlled NASA's money. Brown and Root got the contract to build the space center. The Humble Company developed Clear Lake City on part of the land the company still owned.

Sharpstown Center opened in 1961 as the city's first completely air-conditioned shopping mall. Included in the center was the first suburban Foley's store. Bernard Calkins of Kansas bought the city transit system from the Galveston-Houston Company and introduced the first air-conditioned buses. He called them Dreamliners.

Houston escaped with relatively light damage when Hurricane Carla hit the Texas coast in September, 1961. That storm caused $330 million

47) Pennzoil Place is two separate towers with a common lobby featuring a soaring glass roof.

48) There were happy faces in the Mission Control Center on the July day in 1969 when Astronaut Neil Armstrong radioed from the moon that the spaceship Eagle had landed at Tranquility Base. The man at the far right is Dr. Robert Gilruth, director of the Manned Spacecraft Center at the time. The third man from the right is Dr. Christopher Kraft. He was flight director then and later succeeded Gilruth as head of the center. Kraft was with the space program from the beginning. He complained when he retired in 1982 that the Reagan administration was doing too little to maintain the American lead in space. NASA photograph.

48

damage in the area between Port Arthur and Corpus Christi and exposed Texas television journalists Dan Rather and Tom Jarriel to larger opportunities.

A campaign started by George Kirksey and Craig Cullinan, Jr. in 1956 finally produced a major league baseball franchise for Houston in 1961. Bud Adams, R. E. Bob Smith, and Roy Hofheinz had joined Kirksey and Cullinan in what eventually became the Houston Sports Association. County voters had approved a revenue bond issue to pay for a county stadium. Hofheinz was talking about making it the world's first air-conditioned stadium. But what really got the National League to thinking seriously about expansion was the formation of a third major league. The HSA joined with groups in six other cities in 1959 to form the Continental League. They hired Branch Rickey to head it and then dissolved it in 1960 when the National League and American League agreed to take in some new members. The HSA bought out the Houston Buffs in 1961 after getting a National League franchise. The Houston National League club made its debut in 1962, as the Houston Colt .45s. They played in a temporary stadium on the outer edge of the site that had been chosen by then for the new stadium, which was to be the world's first air-con-

ditioned ball park. County voters approved a $22 million general obliga-
tion bond issue as a substitute for the revenue bond proposal voted earlier,
and voted another $9.6 million general obligation issue in 1962. There
were skeptics but most people wanted to believe Roy Hofheinz's promise
that the stadium would be the Eighth Wonder of the World.

The legislature established the Texas Water Pollution Control Board
in 1961.

Air France began service to Paris from Houston International Airport
in 1962. The bus company went into receivership.

The seven NASA astronauts were welcomed to Houston with a parade
and barbecue on July 4, 1962. The astronauts were celebrities of the first
rank, especially John Glenn because he had just completed the first
American orbital flight. Their arrival validated Houston's "Space City"
status and did wonders for real estate values around Clear Lake.

Oilman John Mecom bought the run-down Warwick apartment hotel
in 1962 and overhauled it, reopening it as a luxury hotel in 1964.

The first section of the 610 Loop was opened to traffic in 1963. It was
the section between Memorial Drive and the Southwest Freeway.

Ben Taub Hospital opened in the Texas Medical Center. This hospital and the older Jeff Davis Hospital on Allen Parkway were operated jointly by the city and county for people unable to pay for hospital care. This arrangement dated from the end of World War I when the Red Cross donated to the city and county the old Camp Logan hospital. This institution soon became inadequate. The city and county built Jeff Davis Hospital on Elder Street in 1925 and then built the new Jeff Davis Hospital in 1938 when the one on Elder became inadequate. Banker and developer Ben Taub was chairman of the city-county hospital board from 1935 until 1964 and it was for him that the new public hospital was named when it opened in 1963.

49) Neil Armstrong made this photograph of Buzz Aldrin placing a seismic experiment package and a laser reflector on the moon in July, 1969. NASA photograph.

50) The name of the original city airport was changed to William P. Hobby Airport when Intercontinental opened in 1969. There were a few quiet months, but Southwest Airlines brought the old terminal back to life in 1971 and the airport was soon busier than it had been when it was the only airport. The terminal is overshadowed by parking garages added since Southwest started flying from here.

50

51) Leon Jaworski of Houston was named Special Prosecutor in the Watergate case in 1973. President Nixon had just fired the original Watergate Prosecutor Archibald Cox. The president's advisers may have thought Jaworski would be disinclined to rock the boat. He was senior partner in a major law firm, a former Chamber of Commerce president, and former president of the American Bar Association. Jaworski had also been an army war crimes prosecutor in Germany. He plunged vigorously into the Watergate investigation. Courtesy Fulbright and Jaworski.

51

The city and county wrangled every year over how much of the public hospitals' cost each government would pay. Four times proposals for the creation of a hospital district to manage the public hospitals were submitted to the voters. Four times they were voted down. The Quaker playwright Jan De Hartog came to town in 1962 to teach at the University of Houston. He volunteered to work as an orderly at Jeff Davis and at Ben Taub. What he wrote in the *Houston Chronicle* and in his book *The Hospital* about seriously sick and wounded people having to wait for hours in crowded and littered rooms and hallways to get medical attention probably helped generate the favorable vote on the hospital district question the fifth time it was presented to the voters in 1965.

The University of Houston was taken into the state university system in 1963.

President John F. Kennedy spent part of the last evening of his life, November 21, 1963, in Houston. The president and Mrs. Kennedy attended a dinner in the Sam Houston Coliseum honoring Congressman Albert Thomas. The president made a speech crediting Thomas with the kind of vision that prevents people from perishing. The Kennedys stayed briefly in the Gold Suite at the Rice Hotel before the dinner but they flew on to spend the night in Fort Worth before flying to Dallas

52

52) By spring of 1974 President Nixon was trying to offset the damage the Watergate scandal was doing to his administration with a series of personal appearances around the country. He fielded questions from reporters and members of the National Association of Broadcasters in Jones Hall the night of March 19. Courtesy Houston Chronicle.

53

53) Two of the correspondents in the
White House Press Corps traveling with
the president at the time were former
Houston TV reporters. Tom Jarriel was
there for ABC. He had formerly worked
at KPRC-TV. The president tried to talk
of other things but the White House
correspondents asked Watergate questions. Courtesy ABC-TV.

54) Dan Rather was the White House
correspondent for CBS-TV. He had
formerly been with KHOU-TV. Some of
President Nixon's staff considered Rather
unfriendly before March 19, 1974. This
perception grew after the president and
Rather bristled at each other on the Jones
Hall stage. The Nixon partisans felt that
Rather "sassed" the president, but the
president did reply to his Watergate
question. Courtesy CBS-TV.

on November 22. Houston adman Jack Valenti had arranged the Thomas
dinner. Vice President Lydon B. Johnson invited him to make the trip
to north Texas with the presidential party. That is how it happened that
Jack Valenti was with Johnson when he was sworn in as president on Air
Force One after Kennedy was killed. Valenti flew on to Washington as
a member of the new president's staff.

Mayor Louie Welch signed an agreement in 1964 for another source
of surface water for the city. The agreement with the Trinity River
Authority provided for development of Lake Livingston. Work began in
1965. The lake was completed in 1969. Hugh Liedtke moved the Pennzoil

54

Company to Houston in 1964. Liedtke had created Pennzoil after buying into the South Penn Oil Company in 1962.

Two high-rise apartment buildings were built downtown in 1965: Houston House, and 2016 Main; but Houstonians did not display any great eagerness to live downtown.

U. S. Steel announced plans in 1965 for a big mill at Baytown that was completed in 1971 and closed in 1987. The legislature created the Texas Air Control Board in 1965.

The firearms people were making noises about getting something in return for allowing the Houston baseball club to use the name Colt .45s, and so the name was changed. Roy Hofheinz was president of the HSA but R. E. Bob Smith owned most of the stock and he was chairman of the board. Apparently Hofheinz decided on his own responsibility to name the club the Astros and call the stadium the Astrodome and this may have helped bring on the showdown between Hofheinz and Smith. Smith said later that their falling out was precipitated by Hofheinz's habit of making decisions without consulting him. The two exchanged views in a meeting that ended with an agreement that one would buy the other out. Smith was to buy Hofheinz's minority interest unless Hofheinz could

55) Donald Bonham and O. C. Mendenhall took over an old Kroger's supermarket on Fulton in the 1970s and established a supermarket with a Latin accent. Their first Fiesta Mart was a big success and they went on to open Fiesta stores all over town. It is the classic success formula. They found something nobody else was doing and did it.

56) Ninfa Laurenzo was a widow with no capital when she started serving Tex-Mex food in 1973 at this little place on Navigation, near downtown. Downtown workers discovered the place and spread the word about Ninfa's tacos. The little restaurant became a chain of restaurants.

find the money to buy Smith's majority interest. Smith never believed that he could, but Hofheinz did arrange to borrow enough money to buy absolute control of the empire. The Astrodome opened the evening of April 9, 1965. The Houston Astros beat the New York Yankees, two to one, in the first game ever played under a plastic roof.

Most people, including Bud Adams, expected that the Houston Oilers would play their home games in the Astrodome, but Adams and Hofheinz could not agree on the rent. Adams arranged, instead, to play at Rice Stadium. He said if the Astrodome was the Eighth Wonder of the World,

57

57) *Indy veteran A. J. Foyt doesn't just race cars, he sells them, and motorcycles, too.*

58) *Herman Brown Park on Mercury Drive off I-10 East was donated to the city by the Brown Foundation in 1979, and named for the co-founder of Brown and Root.*

58

the rent was the ninth. The Oilers played at Rice from 1965 until 1968 when Adams and Hofheinz reached an agreement on the rent.

John Mecom contracted in 1965 to buy the *Houston Chronicle* from Houston Endowment and he was listed for a while as the paper's publisher, but the deal never was consummated.

The National Football League agreed in 1966 to absorb the American Football League and call it the American Conference of the NFL. The AFL clubs agreed to pay $18 million for this favor. John Hollis of the *Houston Post* wrote that it might have been the highest price ever paid for a burial service.

The city started work in 1966 on a new convention center to be named for Albert Thomas, who died in February of that year. The Jesse H. Jones Hall for the Performing Arts opened as the new home of the Houston Symphony, the Houston Grand Opera, and the Houston Ballet. Developer Gerald Hines and Shell Oil announced plans for a new building for Shell. The original plan called for 47 stories but the builders went on up to 50 and One Shell Plaza was the tallest building in town, briefly.

Will Clayton died in 1966 at the age of 86. He had distinguished himself in the diplomatic service as well as in the cotton business. Clayton was Undersecretary of State for Economic Affairs in the 1940s and was credited with originating the Marshall Plan of economic assistance that revived the economy of Europe after World War II.

The city's transit system was bought in 1966 by National City Lines of Florida. Barbara Jordan was elected to the Texas Senate in 1966 after losing races for the House in 1962 and 1964. A realignment of congressional districts in 1966 created a new seat in the U.S. House of Representatives for west Houston and Harris County. George Bush won the right to represent the mostly Republican 7th District and Houston attorney and legislator Bob Eckhart won the election to the District 8 seat that had been occupied by Lera Thomas after Albert Thomas' death.

Air pollution provoked a showdown between the Houston City Hall and the ship channel industries in 1967. The channel never had been annexed to the city. The absence of city taxes and city regulations was one of the inducements that drew industry to the channel. Mayor Louie Welch put the industries on notice that they might be annexed unless they got pollution under control. This threat brought on a series of negotiations and a compromise. The channel plants were allowed to sign agreements with the city making them industrial districts, subject to some city controls, and requiring them to pay some money to the city

59) The most striking Houston example of the phenomenon known as white flight occurred in the Riverside Terrace area. The substantial homes on both sides of Bray's Bayou in this neighborhood were occupied almost exclusively by whites before the 1960s. The presence of Texas Southern University nearby attracted black families. Many of the white residents hurriedly sold out for whatever they could get and moved to the southwestern suburbs. The area is occupied now largely, but not exclusively, by affluent blacks.

60) The Miller Memorial Theater in Hermann Park was originally just a stage. It was built in the 1920s with $50,000 the late Jesse Miller left the city for this purpose. The section of permanent seats, the partial roof, and the backstage area were added later.

in lieu of taxes. If they didn't sign, they would be annexed. Only one refused to sign.

WKY Television Systems of Oklahoma bought Houston's original Ultra High Frequency TV license and put Channel 39 back on the air in 1967 as KHTV. The name of WKY Television Systems was later changed to Gaylord Broadcasting. Channel 39 was licensed originally to the owners of KNUZ Radio. They put KNUZ TV on the air in 1953 and shut it down in 1954. So few Houston TV sets were equipped to receive UHF signals at that time that the station was unable to sell enough advertising to make a profit. The Hofheinz family opened the Astroworld Park in 1967 and also the hotels in what Hofheinz was by this time calling the Astrodomain.

Philip Battlestein's heirs sold the Battlestein stores in 1967 to the Manhattan shirt people. The new owners bought Frost Brothers of San Antonio in 1969. The two chains later merged under the Frost name and then closed in 1989.

61

61) *Roy Hofheinz and others argued in the 1960s that the Astrodome complex was all the convention space Houston needed. But the city built a big new convention center in the downtown civic center area, anyway, and named it for the late Congressman Albert Thomas. Work started in 1966. This center closed when the George R. Brown Convention Center opened and the city council in October of 1991 gave a developer from Maryland a contract to convert it to an entertainment complex.*

62) *The Albert Thomas Convention Center was designed so as not to disturb this old oak tree. This is the Courthouse Oak, also called the Hanging Oak. The county's criminal courthouse stood on this site for 70 years. The tree was right outside the main entrance. Stories have been told about criminals being hanged from the tree but the stories probably are not true.*

62

The Navigation District proposed in 1968 to deepen the channel to 50 feet. Bonds were approved to cover the district's share of the cost but it is not likely all the environmental studies can be completed before 1994.

The National Association of Homebuilders held its convention in the Astrodome complex for the first time in 1969; it was the biggest convention yet for Houston and another triumph for Roy Hofheinz.

Shell announced in 1969 that it would move a substantial part of its headquarters operation from New York to the new Shell buildings in Houston.

Houston Intercontinental Airport opened in June, 1969, and the NASA spaceship *Eagle* reported to Houston on July 20 that it had landed on the moon. A reporter asked one of the NASA officials during the celebration at Clear Lake what time zone the moon was in and the official gloatingly replied, "The moon is on Houston time."

63

63) *The Alley Theater finally got a real home in 1968. Nina Vance moved the theater to this building in the civic center. The late Jesse Jones' Houston Endowment, Incorporated, donated the site. The Ford Foundation put up part of the money for the building. The name was changed* *to Nina Vance Alley Theater after Nina died in 1980. Iris Siff was the director from then until she was murdered in her office in this building in 1982.*

Gerald Hines opened the Galleria at Westheimer and South Post Oak in 1970. Sakowitz and Joske's had built large stores a little earlier at this intersection where there had been only a country store and a vacant school house a few years before.

The Census of 1970 showed a population of 1,232,802 for the city proper, almost double the 1950 population.

Construction began in 1970 on Lake Conroe on the West Fork of the San Jacinto River, another addition to Houston's surface water supply. The lake was completed in 1973. The Gulf Coast Waste Disposal Authority was created in 1970 to encourage and help channel industries to clean up their operations.

Shell Oil bought 500 acres of land near the Astrodome and started a commercial and residential development called Plaza del Oro. Congressman Bush gave up his house seat to make a race for the U.S. Senate. He lost and Bill Archer was elected to succeed him as 7th District congressman.

Work started in 1970 on the Eleven Hundred Milam Building, taller than anything downtown except One Shell Plaza.

One and Two Shell Plaza were completed in 1971 and in the same year two new projects were initiated, both bigger than anything done downtown before. Trammell Crow and the Metropolitan Life Insurance Company started work on Allen Center on an 18-acre site between Smith

Street and Interstate 45 just south of the Civic Center. A big part of this property had been part of the old Fourth Ward slum until the building of the elevated freeway cut it off from the main body of Fourth Ward. Texas Eastern Transmission Company bought up 33 blocks east of Main Street for a development called Houston Center.

Memorial Hospital decided in 1971 to sell its downtown property and move to Sharpstown. Classes began in the new University of Texas Medical School in the Medical Center and the Houston Fire Department took over the operation of emergency ambulances in the city in 1971. Most of the ambulances had previously been operated by undertakers. Some of them deplored the change as a setback for private enterprise.

Leonel Castillo became the first Hispanic to be elected to a citywide office in Houston when he defeated long-time City Controller Roy Oakes in 1971. The new Southwest Airlines brought the Hobby Airport terminal back to life that year. Southwest started with three planes, serving Houston, Dallas, and San Antonio.

The Securities Exchange Commission filed suit in 1971 accusing developer Frank Sharp and several state political figures of stock fraud. The agency charged that some high state officials had been bribed to support banking legislation favored by Sharp. The developer was accused of arranging for the officials to make quick profits by buying and selling stock in his National Bankers' Life Insurance Company. The suit alleged

64) *Dr. Denton Cooley performed the first successful heart transplant operation in America, at St. Luke's Hospital in 1968. Dr. Cooley is a native Houstonian. He grew up in the Heights, and played varsity basketball at the University of Texas. Courtesy Texas Heart Institute.*

65) *Suburbs were spreading around the city's outskirts, but the 1960s also saw a renewed interest in the better, older close-in neighborhoods, like Courtland Place.*

66) *A few of the old mansions that once lined Montrose Boulevard survive but they have mostly gone commercial. There was an esplanade with palm trees down the middle of the boulevard when Mr. and Mrs. Walter Fondren built this home. He was one of the founders of the Humble Company. The family lent the mansion to the Center for the Retarded in 1955 and the Center was here until 1967. The building now houses a restaurant and hotel.*

64

65

66

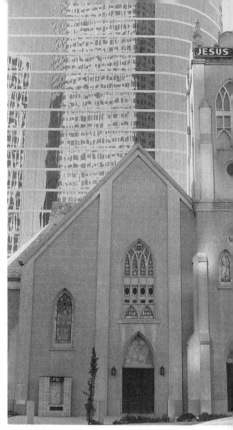

68

67

67) The trend toward downtown developments including several buildings actually started with Cullen Center and continued in the 1970s. Work began in 1971 on the Allen Center development on 18 acres bound by Dallas, Louisiana, Bell, and I-45.

68) Most of the land Allen Center occupies was formerly part of the old Fourth Ward black ghetto. The developers wanted the site occupied by the Antioch Baptist Church but the black congregation firmly resisted all offers and the little church survives, surrounded by glass towers. The man Jack Yates High School was named for was pastor when the Antioch congregation built this building in 1876. Rev. Jack Yates was a former slave, emancipated at the end of the Civil War. He and Rev. Elias Dibble raised the money to buy Emancipation Park in 1872 and maintained it until the city took it over in 1916.

that Sharp's bank lent the politicians the money for the deals. House Speaker Gus Mutscher and two of his aides were convicted of conspiring to accept bribes and the fallout ruined the careers of several other politicians.

Frank Sharp was granted probation and immunity from further prosecution when he pleaded guilty to making a false bank entry and dealing in unregistered stock and agreed to give testimony against the others. The scandal caused a run on his bank. It closed and Sharp lost control of the Sharpstown empire he had created.

Wayne Duddleston, Billy Goldberg, and Ralph O'Connor bought the San Diego Rockets in 1971 and moved them to Houston. This was the first professional basketball franchise in Texas. Raymond Schindler and his associates in Crest Broadcasting Company put KRIV-TV on the air on Channel 26 August 15, 1971. This was the year congress created Amtrak to run what was left of the railroad passenger business.

The Hyatt Regency Hotel opened at Louisiana and Dallas in 1972 and work started on the Pennzoil Building. W. P. Hobby, Jr., son of former Governor W. P. Hobby and Oveta Culp Hobby, was elected lieutenant governor.

The Houston Independent School District established the Houston Community College system in 1972. The system offered classes mostly at night and mostly in the Houston School District's buildings in the beginning.

The port began a major expansion of its Bayport Division in 1972 and oilman George Mitchell started work on his new town at The Woodlands on I-45 North. Mitchell estimated an ultimate investment of $3 billion.

69) *Art patrons John and Dominique de Menil bought a metal sculpture Barnett Newman had created and dedicated to the late Martin Luther King. The de Menils tried to give "The Broken Obelisk" to the city of Houston for display in a public place. But the city declined the offer. The de Menils then, in 1971 built a nondenominational chapel near the University of St. Thomas, decorated the interior with paintings by Mark Rothko, and installed "The Broken Obelisk" in a reflection pool outside. The Rothko Chapel and the sculpture are at Sul Ross and Yupon.*

69

United Gas Company changed its name to Entex in 1972. Entex bought out the Houston distribution system of Houston Natural Gas in 1976 to become the city's only natural gas supplier. Entex became a subsidiary of Arkla in 1988. The Humble Company changed its name and trade mark to Exxon in 1972. The company had adopted Enco as its trade name in 1960 and was marketing its products under that name around the world until it discovered that the meaning of Enco in Japanese was something like "car won't go." Computers were enlisted to find a word that suggested petroleum products but didn't mean anything in any language. Exxon was the word the computers came up with.

70

71

72

70) The Houston Independent School District launched another college in 1972. The Houston Community College has since taken over the old San Jacinto High School building and grounds and this is the main campus of the sprawling and rapidly growing Community College system. It was on this same site that the HISD started the junior college that became the University of Houston. Walter Cronkite was a student here when this was a high school.

71) Louie Welch decided in 1973 not to seek election to a sixth term as mayor. Oscar Holcombe's record of ten terms in the mayor's office still stood, but Welch had set a new record for consecutive terms, at five.

72) The 610 Loop was completed in 1973 when the bridge over the ship channel (background left) opened to traffic. The building in the right foreground is not a real ruin; it is a restaurant built to look like a ruin.

Water pollution was getting a lot of attention in 1972 and the Houston Ship Channel was mentioned more than once as possibly the filthiest body of water in the country. The city itself was identified as the biggest single polluter. Inadequate and overloaded sewage treatment plants were the reason. The city started work on an enormous new sewage treatment plant on the channel at 69th Street and stopped issuing new building permits in areas where the sanitary sewer system was inadequate. The plant was completed in 1983.

The newly created World Hockey Association awarded Houston a hockey franchise in 1972 and Paul Deneau put the Houston Aeros on the ice at Sam Houston Coliseum. The team played there until the Summit opened and then folded in 1978, a year before the WHA merged with the older National Hockey League. Kenneth Schnitzer was the owner of the Aeros when the club folded.

The space base at Clear Lake was named the Lyndon B. Johnson Manned Spacecraft Center in 1973. The legislature approved a bill that year allowing the creation of a Metropolitan Transit Authority, but voters in Houston turned the idea down and the city took over operation of the foundering bus system.

The city was considering a proposal to give a citywide cable TV franchise to a syndicate of business and civic leaders. Opponents forced a referendum and voters vetoed the franchise plan. The leading opponents were the owners of the established television stations.

The first bridge over the ship channel was completed in 1973 as the final link in the 610 Loop system.

President Nixon fired Archibald Cox in 1973 and appointed Leon Jaworski of Houston to be Watergate Special Prosecutor. Jaworski had been a partner in the law firm then known as Fulbright, Crooker, Freeman, and Bates since 1935.

Louie Welch decided not to run for a sixth term after serving an unprecedented five consecutive terms as mayor. Roy Hofheinz's son Fred was elected mayor and Welch was elected president of the Houston Chamber of Commerce in 1974.

The Chamber of Commerce calculated in 1974 that new people were moving to Houston at the rate of 55,000 a year. The Two Houston Center Building was completed in Houston Center that year.

73) The Port of Houston maintains a motor yacht for entertaining prospective customers. The "Sam Houston" also runs regular trips for tourists and the general public. Any one can arrange to make a tour by calling 225-4044. Reservations are required.

74) There are factories and grain elevators, too, but refineries and chemical plants have dominated the banks of the Houston Ship Channel since World War II.

73

74

The only passenger train still using Union Station was switched to the Southern Pacific Station in 1974 and Union Station was closed. The S.P. station off Washington Avenue became the Amtrak Station.

Leon Jaworski prosecuted the Watergate investigation with more vigor than the Nixon White House probably had expected and by 1974 President Nixon was trying to conduct some damage control with appearances around the country.

The president came to Houston on March 19, fresh from a meeting with business executives in Chicago where he had been warmly received. Some of his aides already had been indicted. Jaworski and the House Judiciary Committee were demanding additional tapes and documents Nixon did not want to furnish. He was contending that the doctrine of executive privilege entitled him to withhold the material being demanded. He came to Houston to appear before a group he expected to be every bit as supportive as the people in Chicago. The National Association of Broadcasters was in convention here. The members of this organization are owners and operators of radio and television stations, all holding licenses from the government. No group is less anxious to offend a sitting president.

75

76

75) The Rice Hotel closed in 1977 and the building has been for sale ever since. Real estate people estimated in 1991 that it would take $13 million to buy it and another $40 million to restore it. The Rice is on the site at Texas and Main where the capitol of the Republic of Texas once stood. The late Jesse Jones tore down an earlier, small hotel that had been built on the capitol site and put up the first unit of the present building in 1913.

76) Jeff McKissick died in 1980 at the age of 78 without making any provision for disposition of his life's work. McKissick had spent 20 years transforming his little house at 2401 Munger into a folk art triumph he called The Orange Show. Some critics rank his work with the Watts Tower in Los Angeles. Some of McKissick's fans started a foundation to buy and preserve The Orange Show and keep it open to the public.

158

The president's staff and the broadcasters' organization had arranged a news conference format, where the president would answer questions posed by the broadcasters. The regular White House correspondents were traveling with the president but the president's aides hoped they would not be permitted to ask questions since, as they explained, the White House correspondents had access to the president all the time. The program was staged in Jones Hall. The White House correspondents were permitted to ask questions. Dan Rather was there for CBS. The president and his staff did not consider Rather a friend. When he stood to ask his question, President Nixon just looked at him without inviting him to speak, as he had been doing with others. Rather waited a few seconds and then said, "Mr. President, Dan Rather, CBS News." There was a chorus of boos and some scattered applause from the audience. The president asked, "Are you running for something?" Rather said, "No, Sir, Mr. President, are you?" There were more boos before Rather asked the president to say how the House of Representatives could carry out its duties in the impeachment process if the president continued to hold back evidence the House wanted. The president replied that the House was trying to go beyond the constitutional grounds for impeachment. There were many more questions and answers but the exchange between

77) The Houston Fire Department in 1981 turned old Fire Station Number 7 into a museum. The exhibits include the first water tower the department bought. This machine was built to be pulled by horses. The engine was added when the horses were retired. This station was built at Milam and McIlhenny in 1899. The police department also maintains a museum at the Police Academy building on Aldine-Westfield Road at Rankin.

77

78

78) *Gerald Hines completed work in 1981 on the 70-story Texas Commerce Tower, left. I. M. Pei designed this building.*

79) *Hines went to work the same year on a new building for RepublicBank, designed by Philip Johnson. This was the peak year of the prolonged Houston building boom. The total value of building permits isssued in 1981 was more than $3 billion.*

79

Rather and the president got most of the attention in news accounts of the president's appearance. NBC News President Reuven Frank said Rather smart-assed the president. CBS News President Dick Salant received many demands that he fire Rather. He declined to do it.

The new City Library was completed in the Civic Center in 1975 and the Summit Arena opened in Greenway Plaza. The Summit was built with the proceeds from a city revenue bond issue on land donated by Kenneth Schnitzer. The city owns the building and leases it to an operating company in an arrangement similar to the one between the county and the Houston Sports Association. The Houston Rockets had no regular place to play until the Summit was completed. The Summit also was the home of the Aeros hockey team from 1975 until 1978.

Philanthropist Ima Hogg died in London in 1975 at age 93.

The Houston Rodeo was the biggest in the world by 1975. This was made possible by the Livestock Show and Rodeo's move from the Sam Houston Coliseum to the Astrodome complex in 1966.

Houstonians voted in 1975 to legalize the sale of liquor by the drink, a blow to the private clubs, but a big plus for the restaurant and convention business.

80) Johnson designed a low wing of the Republic Tower, right, to conceal the singularly unattractive building the Western Union Company was occupying at the corner of Capitol and Louisiana. This building, Jones Hall, The Alley, and the Albert Thomas Convention Center all face Jones Plaza in the Civic Center named for the late longtime Houston mayor Oscar F. Holcombe.

80

The legislature created the Coastal Subsidence District in 1975 to begin regulating and reducing the withdrawal of groundwater in Harris and Galveston counties.

Howard Hughes, Jr. died on April 5, 1976, on a chartered jet that was bringing him to the Texas Medical Center. He was 71 and a billionaire. He had been a recluse for 13 years, living in Las Vegas, the Bahamas, and Mexico, where he was when he lapsed into the coma that prompted his staff to try to get him to the medical center.

Congressman Bob Casey resigned in 1976 to accept appointment to the National Maritime Commission. Republican Ron Paul of Lake Jackson was elected to succeed him.

The One Houston Center building in Houston Center was completed in 1977. Work started that year on the First International Bank Tower where Memorial Hospital had been.

The National Women's Conference was held in Houston in November, 1977. It was part of the observance of International Women's Year and it was the biggest women's meeting ever held in America. Former Congresswoman Bella Abzug of New York was in the chair and the delegates resolved among other things that the Equal Rights Amendment ought to be ratified.

81) No one can say with certainty what Houston would look like if there had been zoning from the start. But Smith Street has become one of the handsomest commercial thoroughfares in North America without zoning.

81

162

82) A tunnel system including shops and eating places links most of the newer downtown buildings and some of the older ones. The system is more than six miles long. It is possible to walk from Allen Center on the west side of downtown to Houston Center on the east side without leaving the tunnel system and without suffering from lack of refreshments.

82

City Council member Jim McConn was elected mayor of Houston in 1977 and the city the same year annexed Clear Lake City and some other large suburban areas, including Alief.

British Caledonian Airways started direct service between Houston and London in 1977. The city transit system established the first Park and Ride service on the Gulf Freeway and started planning contraflow lanes for buses on the freeways. Voters in 1978 approved the creation of a Metropolitan Transit Authority to take over the bus system. Also approved was a one-cent addition to the sales tax to pay for improvements to the system. The first contraflow lane opened, on I-45 North, in 1979. It worked better than some people had expected. There was only one fatal accident on it in the first 5 years.

The Chamber of Commerce reported that 539 energy companies had headquarters in Houston by 1978.

Tranquility Park in the Civic Center was completed in 1979 and the city council that year granted cable TV franchises for separate areas of the city to five groups made up chiefly of people with political influence. The franchisees soon sold their rights to the national chains, Warner and Storer.

163

83) *Most of the new buildings built in Houston between the 60s and the 80s were built on sites where older buildings had been. Few concerns profited more from the building boom than the demolishing company the late Immanuel "Wrecker" Olshan founded in 1933.*

84) *There were no black officers in the upper echelons of the Houston Police Department before 1982 when Mayor Kathy Whitmire surprised the department by naming Lee Brown to the chief's job. Brown came here from the chief's job in Atlanta. Courtesy Houston Police Department.*

83

The port reported a new record of 112,056,767 tons of cargo handled during 1979.

Work started in 1979 on the Texas Commerce Tower. The value of building permits issued by the city for the year 1979 went above $2 billion for the first time. Almost three times as much office space was built in the 1970s as was built in the 1960s.

The number of vehicles in the city almost doubled between 1970 and 1979. City officials and civic leaders have been busy ever since trying to fend off Environmental Protection Agency moves to limit industrial building permits and restrict the use of motor vehicles.

The city council proposed a charter amendment in August, 1979 to expand the number of council positions from eight to 14, to comply with the 1964 Voting Rights Act requiring more minority representation. Nine of the 14 council members were to be elected by district and the district boundaries were drawn to make it likely that some blacks and Hispanics would be elected. Moses LeRoy had filed a suit in federal court to force redistricting and the city government wanted to hold a bond election, but the Department of Justice was not going to allow that without some move toward compliance with the Voting Rights Act. City voters approved the expansion. The bond issues were approved in Sep-

164

84

tember and the city council election was held in November. The council had always been all-male. It had been all-white from the end of Reconstruction until 1971 when black real estate operator Judson Robinson was elected. Robinson was reelected and two more black men were elected in 1979, Ernest McGowen and Anthony Hall. Also elected were the council's first women members, Eleanor Tinsley and Christin Hartung, both white, and the first Hispanic, Ben Reyes. The Astros signed free agent Nolan Ryan in 1979.

The Census of 1980 showed a population of 1,594,086 for Houston. Only New York, Chicago, Los Angeles, and Philadelphia had bigger numbers and Houston passed Philadelphia in 1982, by unofficial Houston calculations.

A survey of new office buildings in 1981 revealed that more new office space was built in the suburbs than was built downtown during the preceding five years. *Houston Magazine* listed 54 suburban office parks, but building continued downtown, too. The Texas Commerce Tower was completed in 1981. Work was proceeding on the Capital National Plaza in Allen Center, on the First City Tower, on 1010 Lamar, and on 801 Travis. The old Memorial Professional Building on Louisiana was being demolished to make way for the new Allied Bank Tower. Building permits totalled $2.5 billion in 1980.

The city bought the old Sharpstown Country Club and began convert-
ing it to a public park. The city council agreed to make the two blocks
bound by Texas Avenue, Smith, Preston, and the bayou available for a
proposed new Lyric Theater. George Brown was pushing for a new and
bigger convention hall in Houston Center.

Work began in 1981 on the Allied Bank Tower, and on a new Gulf
Tower and The Park retail mall, both in Houston Center. A new hotel
was completed in Allen Center, originally called the Meridian and operated originally by Air France.

American General started work on a new 42-story tower in the American General Center in 1981. Gerald Hines started work on a new tower
for Republic Bank on the block bound by Smith, Capitol, Louisiana,
and Rusk. Hines bought the Lamar Hotel block bound by Main, McKinney, Travis, and Lamar. He closed the hotel in 1983, sold the contents,
and in 1985 demolished the Lamar and the other buildings on the block,
including the remnants of the long-closed Loew's and Metropolitan, once
the city's grandest movie palaces. Hines started work on a new building
for Transco near the Galleria. The Transco Tower was the tallest building
outside the downtown district when it was completed in 1983. Building
permits issued in 1981 added up to $3 billion. It was the largest total

*85) Gulf Oil moved from the venerable
Gulf Building on Main in 1983 to the
new Gulf Tower in Houston Center.
Chevron bought out Gulf in a $13 billion
deal the following year and this became
the Chevron Tower.*

85

86) *Gerald Hines bought the Lamar Hotel block in 1983 and demolished all the buildings, including the old C&I Life Building and what was left of Loew's State and the Metropolitan Theater. The block became a parking lot.*

86

recorded in a single year by any American city up to that time. The port was again third in the nation in total tonnage handled, and first in foreign trade.

The board of the Houston Independent School District was expanded from seven members to nine members in 1981 for the same reason the city council had been expanded.

The city election in the fall of 1981 produced something new. Mayor Jim McConn failed to make the runoff. City Controller Kathy Whitmire beat former sheriff Jack Heard to become the first woman mayor in the city's history. She made some changes. She hired Alan Kiepper away from Atlanta to run the Metro system and she brought Lee Brown from Atlanta to be chief of police. Brown was the city's first black police chief.

The Texas Turnpike Authority completed a toll bridge over the ship channel at Beltway 8 in 1982 and named it for the late Jesse Jones. Channel 20, Inc., put KTXH-TV on the air on Channel 20 on November 7, 1982.

Roy Hofheinz died on November 21, 1982 at the age of 70. Most of the empire he had created had gotten away from him a few years before.

87

He couldn't meet the payments on the debts he had incurred in buying control of the HSA and building hotels and the Astroworld Park. His creditors foreclosed in 1975. G. E. Credit and Ford Motor Credit Company took control and then sold HSA and the hotels to a limited partnership headed by John McMullen in 1979. The Hofheinz funeral procession detoured to circle the Astrodome enroute to Glenwood Cemetery on November 24, 1982.

Caroline Hunt's Rosewood Corporation built the Remington Hotel on Briar Oaks Lane for a reported $60 million in 1982. Investors from out of state bought it six years later for half that price and changed the name to Ritz-Carlton. The Queen of England and Prince Philip stayed at the Ritz-Carlton when they visited Houston in May, 1991.

The Four Seasons Hotel in Houston Center was completed in 1982, as were several high-rise condominium buildings. Plans were announced for the 50-story Four Allen Center. Work started on the United Bank Plaza Building at 1415 Louisiana and on the 1600 Smith Building in Cullen Center. But applications for new building permits fell a little short of the 1981 mark.

Houston Democrat Mark White upset Republican Governor Bill Clements in the November election in 1982 and when White took office in 1983, he named Houston developer Bob Lanier to chair the Texas Highway Commission. Lanier held that job until Clements won the governor's office back in 1986. Houston did not lack for highway improvements.

George Bush had served in several high appointive offices during the Nixon and Ford administrations and then returned to Houston when the

87) The Harris County Heritage Society got architect Alfred C. Finn's original rendering of the buildings and the numbers from the door to the Lamar Hotel suite where the rich and mighty met for so many years.

88) 8-F host George R. Brown had died shortly before Hines bought the Lamar and there were few people left in Houston with the kind of clout the people who met in 8-F had.

88

Democrats captured the White House in 1976. The Bushes were living on Indian Trail on the west side when he mounted his campaign for the Republican presidential nomination in 1982. They sold the house on Indian Trail and moved to Washington after he was elected vice president in November, but the vice president continued to vote in Texas, as he said he had since 1948.

Democratic State Representative Clint Hackney challenged Bush's qualifications for voting in Texas but attorney Hal DeMoss argued that the vice president still considered Texas his home and Tax Collector Carl Smith, as voting registrar, ruled on June 3, 1985, that it was okay for Bush to continue voting here.

Houston and Harris County got another congressional district in 1982 and Assistant District Attorney Mike Andrews, a Democrat, was elected to represent the new District 25.

Applications for building permits were back down by 1983 to the 1978 level, below $2 billion. The petroleum industry was in a slump. Business declined at the port. Migration from the North and East dwindled. Real estate brokers were estimating that it might take two years for the developers of office buildings already built to find tenants to fill them. The rest of the country and the rest of Texas appeared to think this was just a local problem. Speculative building continued elsewhere, and even in Houston, until the savings and loans started crashing in 1986.

Metro proposed to begin a rail system from the southwest suburbs to downtown with provisions for later extensions. Voters rejected the plan in an election held on June 11, 1983. Metro started planning more improvements to the bus system and more contraflow lanes. Harris County Judge Jon Lindsay and Commissioners Court easily won voter approval for a County Toll Road Authority. The authority completed the Hardy Street Toll Road from 610 North to Intercontinental Airport and I-45 North in June, 1988, and the Sam Houston Tollway between the Southwest Freeway and I-45 North in July, 1990.

City voters in 1983 approved plans for the new convention hall George Brown wanted in Houston Center. Brown did not live to see it but it was named for him when it opened in September, 1987.

Houstonian Frank Lorenzo changed the character of the airline business in 1983 when he put Continental Airlines in bankruptcy and reorganized the company, voiding union contracts in the process. Lorenzo had acquired Continental in 1981 and merged it with the regional Texas International he had acquired in 1972.

The federal government deeded Ellington Field to the city in 1984. The city did not change the name.

Jerry Argovitz and his partners fielded a Houston team in the new United States Football League in 1984. The Houston Gamblers played their home games in the Astrodome until Argovitz and company sold them in 1985 to Eastern interests who moved them to New Jersey. Jack Pardee was the Gamblers' coach.

The Getty Oil Company of California agreed in 1984 to merge with Pennzoil of Houston, then merged instead with Texaco. Pennzoil filed suit for damages.

The Market Square Historic District on Main Street was entered in the National Register of Historic Places in 1984. One of the district buildings most cherished by preservationists collapsed the same year. The Pillot Building on Congress Avenue was put back up by a syndicate called City Partnership Limited.

Oil prices were dropping in 1985 toward a low of around $10 a barrel by 1986. Many investors were ruined, oil service concerns were folding, drilling rigs were stacked, loans were going into default, and property values in Houston were declining. Appraised tax valuations in the county totalled $132.8 billion in 1985 and they declined by $16 billion between 1985 and 1990, when they turned up again.

Houston Natural Gas merged with InterNorth of Omaha in 1985, and adopted the name Enron Corporation. Enron established headquarters in a Schnitzer building at 1400 Smith. HNG chairman Kenneth Lay became Enron's chairman.

A jury in Houston in 1985 found in favor of Pennzoil in the damage suit Pennzoil had filed against Texaco over the Getty merger. The jury

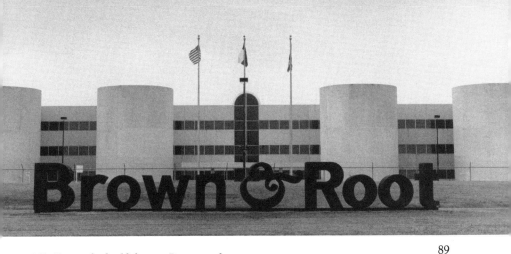

89) *Brown had sold the vast Brown and Root construction empire to Halliburton in 1962, the same year Herman Brown died. This is still one of the biggest engineering and construction firms in the world.*

awarded Pennzoil $11 billion in damages. Texaco set appeals in motion but settled with Pennzoil two years later for $3 billion.

One of the area's high-flying real estate speculators was brought down in 1987. His creditors forced J. R. McConnell into Chapter 11. His obligations were said to be around $500 million and he was accused of swindling investors. McConnell was indicted in 1987 and he killed himself in the Harris County Jail in July, 1988.

The explosion of the *Challenger* on January 28, 1986, put NASA's flight schedules on a prolonged hold.

The owners of KTRK TV, the Capital Cities chain, bought the ABC television network in 1986. The city of Houston upset environmentalists by buying 1,432 acres of prairie in Waller County for a proposed fourth airport. The price of the land, south of I-10 West between Katy and Brookshire, in an area much favored by migratory geese, was $5.7 million.

Billy Reagan retired in 1986 from his position as Superintendent of the Houston schools and the school board picked Joan Raymond, superintendent of the Yonkers system in New York to replace him. Dr. Raymond was the first woman to head the Houston district.

Both the surviving Houston daily newspapers changed hands in 1987. Houston Endowment sold the *Houston Chronicle* to the Hearst Corporation. The *Toronto Sun* sold the *Houston Post* to Dean Singleton's Media News Group.

171

Dr. Paul Chu of the University of Houston achieved overnight fame with a breakthrough that could lead to development of a conducting material with no resistance to electricity.

Joske's sold out to Dillard's and disappeared from the Houston scene in 1987. Dillard's closed some of the stores and changed the name of the others.

The Texas Medical Center demolished the Shamrock Hotel in 1987. The center had bought the hotel and grounds from Hilton in 1985 and then determined that the hotel building could not be converted to serve its purposes. The parking garage and the Grand Ballroom were saved. The swimming pool was covered with a parking lot.

The theater that was being called the Lyric when it was in the planning phase got a new name when the foundation established by insurance magnate Gus Wortham made a large donation to the building fund. The Wortham Theater was completed and opened in May, 1987. A new art museum was completed the same year on Sul Ross in the St. Thomas University neighborhood to house the treasures collected by Schlumberger heiress Dominique de Menil and her husband John.

Respected old Texas banks were buying each other and merging to try to avoid being swamped by loans they could not collect. Bank of the Southwest merged with Mercantile of Dallas to become MBank in 1984. The venerable Texas Commerce sold out to Chemical of New York in

90) A new hotel opened in an old building downtown in 1983. Lancaster Partners, Limited, bought the old Auditorium Hotel at 701 Texas Avenue, turned it into an upscale hotel, and named it the Lancaster. The Auditorium Hotel was built in 1926 facing the old Houston City Auditorium, which was demolished in 1965 to make way for Jones Hall.

91) The Menil Collection is a museum built to house the vast art collection assembled by Dominique de Menil and her late husband John. The Menil Foundation built the museum in the 1500 block of Sul Ross and opened it in 1987.

91

1987. United Bank and Western Bank both failed in 1987 and First City was reorganized with federal assistance. RepublicBank merged with Inter-First in 1987 to become First Republic.

Loans he could not pay off forced former Governor John Connally into bankruptcy in 1988. The Connallys raised $2.5 million for their creditors by selling their personal possessions. John and Nellie Connally attended every session of the auction at Hart Galleries, visiting with the bidders and buyers.

The last downtown skyscraper built before the end of the boom bank-rupted the developers who had paid the highest price yet for downtown property. A partnership including the Michigan State Employees Pension System bought the Heritage Plaza on Bagby for a reported $110 million in 1988, rented most of it to Texaco in 1989 and changed the name to Texaco Heritage Plaza.

Merger did not save First Republic Bank. The new company failed in July of 1988 and NCNB Corporation of North Carolina took it over with federal assistance. The Houston Astros balked at his asking price and declined to offer Nolan Ryan a new contract in 1988. He went on to greater fame and bigger paychecks with the Texas Rangers.

Mayor Whitmire appointed former Highway Commission Chairman Bob Lanier to chair the Metro board in 1988. Voters the same year approved Metro's Phase Two Mobility Plan including a rail line.

Defense attorney Percy Foreman died August 25, 1988 at the age of 86. Foreman grew up in Lufkin where his father was sheriff. Watching trials convinced him he should be a lawyer. He started work in Houston

173

92) The outdoor Cullen Sculpture Garden at the Museum of Fine Arts opened in 1986. It was designed by Japanese sculptor Isamu Noguchi.

93) Dozens of Houston banks failed between 1985 and 1990. Some of the small bank buildings were turned into eateries. This one just fell down in 1991. Fallbrook National, on Farm Road 1960, had failed in 1989. One hundred and thirty-four bank failures were recorded in Texas that year.

as an assistant district attorney but soon switched to defense work and became a star. Cases he tried always drew crowds of spectators. He gained a national reputation for getting defendants acquitted, so people in serious trouble beat a path to his door and made him rich. He never denied that his fees were high. He often said, "My fees are their punishment." But he also defended people without money and from them he accepted whatever they had. He ended up with more jewels, houses, and cars than he could count. The criminal courts in Harris County shut down for Percy Foreman's funeral.

His cherished Shamrock Hotel was shut down and gone when the once flamboyant wildcatter Glenn McCarthy died on December 26, 1988, 81 years and one day after he was born.

The Houston Chamber of Commerce had become the Greater Houston Chamber of Commerce by the time Eileen T. Crowley became president in December, 1988. She was the chamber's first female president. The chamber merged with the Economic Development Council in 1989 to form the Greater Houston Partnership. The Houston World Trade Council joined the partnership in July, 1989. All three organizations still exist as divisions of the Greater Houston Partnership.

Bank failures continued. MBank became insolvent and was reborn as Bank One, still occupying the original Bank of the Southwest quarters on Travis.

Panhandle Eastern took over Texas Eastern Transmission in a $3 billion deal in February, 1989, and sold off the Houston Center development in December. The buyers were JMB-Houston Center Partners. Panhandle Eastern had started in Kansas in 1929 and moved to Houston in 1967.

Congressman Mickey Leland was killed August 7, 1989, in a plane crash in Ethiopia. State Senator Craig Washington won the special election to succeed Leland in the district originally represented by Barbara Jordan.

An explosion and fire at the Phillips plant in Pasadena killed 23 workers in October, 1989, and the first of the famous Houston oilwell firefighters died the same year, at the age of 100. He was H. L. Pat Patton. He had started his career in 1929.

The Wyndham Hotel chain took over the Warwick Hotel and started another renovation in 1989. John Mecom, Jr. had surrendered the hotel to his creditors in 1987.

The city council imposed admission fees at the Hermann Park Zoo for the first time in 1989.

Houston got a new passenger train service in 1989 when Franklin Denson, with a lot of support from Galveston interests, started running the Texas Limited between Houston and the island, on weekends. But commuter rail proposals continued to generate controversy. During the mayoral election campaign in the fall of 1989 when Mayor Whitmire was being challenged by former mayor Fred Hofheinz, Bob Lanier let it

93

94

94) Joan Raymond succeeded Billy Reagan as General Superintendent of the Houston Independent School District in 1986 and held the job for five years. She came from a superintendent's job in New York state and took a superintendent's job in Illinois when the Houston school board decided it was time for another change. Courtesy Houston Independent School District.

95) The wreckers attacked the Shamrock Hotel in 1987 to make way for expansion of the Texas Medical Center. The Center had bought the hotel from the Hilton chain in 1986.

96) The legendary criminal defense lawyer Percy Foreman died in Houston September 25, 1988 at the age of 86. Foreman, left, was still king of the hill when he and Richard "Racehorse" Haynes both spoke at a 1966 Houston Bar Association meeting. Haynes was beginning to enjoy some major successes as a defense attorney himself and Foreman told the audience, "I taught Haynes everything he knows, but I didn't teach him everything I know." Courtesy Richard "Racehorse" Haynes.

97) Elizabeth Watson was appointed chief of police in 1990 when Chief Lee Brown left to take the police commissioner's job in New York City. She joined the police force in 1972 and rose to the rank of captain in command of the Westside Station before Mayor Whitmire named her to the chief's job. She is the first woman to head a big city police department. Her husband is a sergeant on the force. Courtesy Houston Police Department.

95

96   97

be known that he was not enthusiastic about Metro's rail plans. He talked about resigning from his post as Metro chairman. Mayor Whitmire and her supporters persuaded him to stay. With this apparent vote of confidence, Lanier then forced the resignation of Metro's pro-rail general manager, Alan Kiepper. But Mayor Whitmire fired the last shot in this skirmish, after she won reelection. She let Lanier know he was not going to be reappointed to the chairman's job. Lanier quit. Kiepper got a better job as head of the New York transit system and the Metro rail plan was still alive.

A trivia question making the rounds after the 1989 city election was "Name the only living ex-mayor Kathy Whitmire has not beaten." She defeated Jim McConn to get elected the first time in 1981. She beat back a challenge by former mayor Louie Welch in 1985. C. A. Neal Pickett was the only living ex-mayor who had never opposed her and he died March 22, 1990. Pickett had served one term as mayor, 1940-1942.

Two black women won seats on the city council in the election of 1989. Sheila Jackson Lee was elected to a seat that had been occupied by black men since 1979. Beverly Clark defeated a white male council member, Jim Westmoreland.

The 1990 Census put the population of Houston proper at 1,630,553. Local officials complained that the census takers missed more than 85,000 residents but Commerce Secretary Robert Mosbacher refused to adjust the numbers. The increase over the 1980 Census, within the city limits, was only about 36,000. The increase for the county as a whole was more

98

98) The city's oldest civil rights activist died in 1990 at the age of 96. Christia Adair was widely respected as an advisor to generations of black people, a longtime precinct judge and a pillar of the N.A.A.C.P. She is pictured here, left, discussing with Dr. John Biggers a mural he was doing on her life for the southeast Harris County park named for her.

99) Some major Houston buildings are named for two of the black civil rights activists of the 1960s. The Houston School Board named a new high school at 5800 Eastex Freeway for Barbara Jordan in 1980. The main post office building is also named for the retired Congresswoman.

than 400,000 to a 1990 total of 2,818,199. Real estate values were rising again but the prolonged recession of the 1980s and competition from big name national chains ruined one of the city's major retailers. The last Sakowitz store closed in 1990. Simon and Tobias Sakowitz had brought their Sakowitz store to Houston from Galveston in 1911. Tobias's son Bernard and his son Robert expanded the business to 18 stores before the company went into bankruptcy in 1985.

The Port of Houston handled a record 125 million tons of cargo in 1990. The Harris County Hospital District opened two new hospitals: another Ben Taub in the Medical Center, and the Lyndon B. Johnson

Hospital on the north side. The original Ben Taub and the 1938 Jeff Davis were closed.

The famous Gilley's honky-tonk in Pasadena was demolished in 1990 after being damaged by fire. The place had been closed because of a dispute and lawsuit between Mickey Gilley and his partner Sherwood Cryer.

County Commissioner E. A. "Squatty" Lyons retired in 1990 after a record 48 years in office. Republican Jerry Eversole won the election to succeed Lyons and brought about a Republican majority on the Harris County Commissioners Court for the first time since Reconstruction. The other members were County Judge Jon Lindsay and Commissioner Steve Radack, Republicans, and Commissioner Jim Fonteno and Commissioner El Franco Lee, Democrats.

President Bush and the leaders of the world's other major economic powers held their 1990 Economic Summit meeting at Rice University. Rice and the University of Houston, too, were lobbying energetically for the Bush Presidential Library. Both schools were surprised when the president announced in 1991 that his library would be located at Texas A&M. But Houston boosters got something to cheer about when the Republican National Committee announced January 8, 1991 that the party's

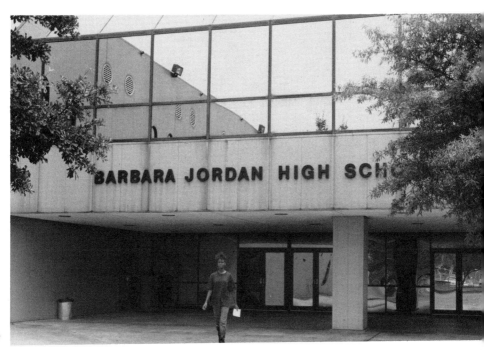

99

100

101

100) The new international terminal at Intercontinental Airport was named when it opened in 1990 for the late Congressman Mickey Leland. The federal office building on Smith Street is also named for Leland.

101) The Texas Parks and Wildlife Department completed a multimillion dollar restoration of the battleship Texas in 1990 and returned the ship to the San Jacinto Battleground where it is open to visitors every day. The U.S. Navy donated the retired battleship to the state in 1948.

102) Real estate man Gary Warwick saved the last downtown movie house. He renovated it, turned it into a party room, renamed it the Majestic Metro, and reopened it in May, 1991. This was originally the Ritz Theater, built by the Scanlan sisters in 1926 and operated for many years by the late showman Will Horowitz.

102

1992 national convention would be held in the Astrodome, fulfilling one of the prophecies Roy Hofheinz made before the dome was built.

Officials of the Port of Houston and Galveston officials started talking in 1991 about the possibility that the Port of Houston might buy the Port of Galveston.

Most members of the board of the Houston Independent School District had seemed to be pleased with Superintendent Joan Raymond before but by 1991 some of them were saying she was too authoritarian. They forced her to resign, paid off her contract, and hired the more convivial Frank Petruzielo of Florida to take her place. Dr. Raymond moved on to another superintendent's job in Illinois.

The new Texas Racing Commission in 1991 awarded Sam Houston Race Park Ltd. a license to build a racetrack in northwest Harris County. This was the first Class 1 license issued by the commission established after Texas voters in 1987 approved a constitutional amendment to legalize pari-mutuel betting. Betting on horse races had been banned in 1909, legalized in 1933, and banned again in 1937.

103

103) Some of the old commercial buildings in the warehouse district around Wood and Walnut streets on the north bank of the bayou, downtown, are being turned into studios and apartments. Not quite everybody is determined to live in the suburbs.

104) People so inclined can join just about any of the many private clubs in Houston if they have the money and some members to sponsor them. But they might wait quite a long time at the Bayou Club, where the membership is made up almost exclusively of old Houston families. The Bayou Club is on the northern edge of Memorial Park. The Houston Polo Club plays regular games in the spring and fall on a field nearby. The polo field is visible from I-10 but it is not open to the public.

104

105) The Texas Medical Center reached new heights in 1991 with the completion of the St. Luke's Medical Tower, left, designed by Cesar Pelli. At 29 stories, the St. Luke's Tower dominates the medical center skyline.

106) Harris County completed a big new jail in 1991 (right). This building on the north bank of Buffalo Bayou, opposite Allen's Landing, was previously a cold storage warehouse. Sheriff Johnny Klevenhagen says this is the biggest single jail building in the country.

The building on the left was called the Merchants and Manufacturers', or M & M Building, when it was built in 1928. It is now the home of the University of Houston Downtown school.

105

106

10[

10[

107) Senators Phil Gramm and Lloyd Bentsen, Congressmen Jack Brooks and Mike Andrews, Mayor Kathy Whitmire, and Harris County Judge Jon Lindsay joined space officials in breaking ground in 1991 for a new building at the base to house a visitors' center and exhibits.

108) Kathy Whitmire equaled Louie Welch's record of five consecutive terms as mayor and made a vigorous campaign in 1991 for a sixth term, opposed by Bob Lanier and black legislator Sylvester Turner. She failed to make the runoff but set a record of sorts. Nobody before had run for a sixth consecutive term.

109) The Veterans Administration completed a new hospital near the medical center in 1991, replacing the V. A. Hospital originally built by the navy in 1946.

184

The 1990 Census required a realignment of the Houston City Council district boundaries. Minority groups anxious to get more minority members on the council persuaded the legislature to require an election on a proposal to expand the council from five members elected at large and nine members elected by districts to six at-large members and 16 district members. Voters rejected this proposal emphatically on August 10, 1991.

Kathy Whitmire made a bid for a record sixth consecutive terms as mayor but it failed. State Representative Sylvester Turner captured most of the black votes in the election in November, 1991. Deposed Metro Chairman Bob Lanier drew most of the conservative vote. Both men campaigned against an expensive monorail plan being pushed by the mayor and a majority of the Metro board. Mayor Whitmire ran third. Bob Lanier beat Sylvester Turner in the runoff and took over the mayor's job in January, 1992.

The legislature in 1991 consolidated all the air and water pollution agencies into a new entity called the Texas Natural Resources Conservation Commission. The act included a provision requiring the city of Houston to furnish water and sewer service by 1996 to areas already annexed to the city. A few areas had been within the city limits and without basic services for years. But the city annexed relatively little new territory after Kathryn Whitmire took over the mayor's office in 1982. The Voting Rights Act of 1964 prohibits dilution of minority voting strength. Whites predominate in most of the areas eligible for

109

110) The Houston International Festival in 1991 spotlighted the culture and art of Japan. This festival started as a small street party in 1977 and grew larger each year. It took the name Houston Festival in 1980 and became the Houston International Festival in 1987. Sponsors are the National Endowment for the Arts, the Texas Commission for the Arts, the Cultural Arts Council of Houston, business firms, and individuals. The 1992 Festival focuses on the art and culture of Spain.

annexation. Annexing them would bring on trouble of the kind most elected officials go out of their way to avoid.

The emphasis shifted from expansion to management of the area the city already occupies. Councilman Jim Greenwood resurrected the idea of zoning in 1990. The City Council in January, 1991, changed the name of the Planning Commission to Planning and Zoning Commission and told the renamed agency to devise a zoning plan for what has long been the biggest unzoned city in North America.

The swashbucklers are all gone. The big banks are owned by people somewhere else and the influx of people from somewhere else has altered the atmosphere and attitude of Houston.

The place the late columnist Hubert Mewhinney referred to as a "whiskey and trombone town" has more joggers than whiskey drinkers and more mariachis than trombones.

PART FOUR

Color
Photographs

Identification of color photographs on the following pages.

P 191   The downtown office buildings tower over tiny Sam Houston Park, the original
        Houston city park.

P192   Above: Sam Houston Park is the focal point of most of the city's many
        celebrations and festivals.
        Middle: The water wall in the Galleria was created by Phillip Johnson. It
        complements the Transco Building Johnson designed in 1981 for Gerald Hines.
        Below: The fountains in Tranquility Park in the downtown civic center disguise
        air vents for the parking garage beneath this park, which commemorates the
        1969 moon landing.

P 193   Above: The fountain in Sam Houston Park is a refreshment stand for the horses
        of the mounted police patrol. This may be the oldest functioning fountain in the
        city. It was originally installed on the grounds of the T. H. Scanlan home
        at 1917 Main, about 1892.
        Middle: There was some criticism in 1954 when the city let John Mecom plow
        up a sunken garden in the traffic circle at South Main and Montrose to install the
        Mecom fountain in its place. Mecom was refurbishing the Warwick Hotel
        at the time.
        Below: Memorial Drive follows Buffalo Bayou westward from downtown and
        this is the route most favored by the sponsors of marathons and fun-run events.
        This part of Memorial Drive is often closed to other traffic on weekends.

P194   Above: The critics were heard from again when the Texas Medical Center and
        the Wortham Foundation created this fountain walk in 1991 on the former
        Shamrock Hotel property which has become an extension of the Medical Center.
        Below: The view of the downtown skyline from I-45 North at twilight is a sight
        many Houston commuters see only in their rearview mirrors.

P 195   Above: The Transco Tower, at 64 floors, is said to be the tallest suburban office
        building in the country.
        Below: Most of the city's fountains are purely decorative. This one screens the
        driveway entrance to the Tenneco Building from Louisiana Street.

P 196   Above: Fountains and a sundial enhance the entrance to the Houston Museum
        of Natural Science and Burke Baker Planetarium. The planetarium was
        financed mostly by insurance executive Burke Baker, who died shortly before it
        was completed in 1964.
        Middle: The Texas Medical Center may be on the way to becoming the city's
        greatest single asset. The center in 1992 counts 41 institutions and more than
        50,000 employees and is the largest concentration of medical care and research
        institutions in the world. It was founded with money made from cotton handled
        through the port.

188

Below: M. D. Anderson Hospital acquired this fountain in 1974 when it took over the Holcombe Boulevard building originally built for the Prudential Insurance Company in 1950.

P 197 Above: The biggest sports stadium in town is on the campus of Rice University, with 70,000 seats. The 1974 Superbowl game was played here. The Astrodome couldn't accommodate the 71,882 fans who came to see Miami beat Minnesota 24-7.
Middle: There are a few reminders, even inside the Loop, of the way people lived in Houston before freeways, shopping malls, and air-conditioning.
Below: The land for what became Hermann Park was donated to the city by George Hermann shortly before he died in 1914.

P 198 Above left: And there are still some producing oil wells in the immediate environs of the city that remains the petrochemical technology capital of the world.
Above right: The Houston Oilers pay rent to the Houston Sports Association when they play in the Dome. The Oilers played elsewhere until 1968 because Oilers' owner Bud Adams thought the rent was too high.
Below left: The Astrodome has been the home of the National League Houston Astros since 1965. The Houston Sports Association owns the Astros and holds the lease on the building, which is owned by Harris County.
Below right: The fountain American General founder Gus Wortham installed on Allen Parkway opposite his American General Center was copied from one Wortham had admired in Australia. It turned out to be easy to get a duplicate. The Australian fountain had been built by Brown and Root of Houston. This center was taking shape in Wortham's mind 30 years before building started. Wortham began buying the land in the 1930s.

P 199 Above: This fountain surrounds a statue of George Hermann, installed in 1981 on the corner of Hermann Park facing the hospital Hermann's money built. There was a free campground for travelers in Hermann Park in the 1920s. Some towns in West Texas still maintain free campgrounds for tourists. Houston does not.
Middle: One of the several fountains in the Texas Medical Center. The building in the background is one of the new wings of Methodist Hospital.
Below: Memorial Park was developed in the 1920s on the site of the World War I army base that had been called Camp Logan. The army had a modest golf course at the camp but the present golf course in Memorial was built in 1936 by the WPA.

P 200 Above: Goodyear maintains a base for one of its blimps off I-45 North at Holzwarth Road. This base was established in 1969. The company moved the blimp to a new home in Ohio in 1992.

189

Middle: *The last big Houston project promoted by George R. Brown was not built until after he died. Brown wanted the city to build a new convention hall in the Houston Center development his Texas Eastern Company had established. The Astrodome interests opposed the idea and some members of City Council questioned the location. But the hall Brown wanted was built where he wanted it and it was named the George R. Brown Convention Center when it opened in 1987.*

Below: *The space base at Clear Lake was given the name Lyndon B. Johnson Manned Spacecraft Center in 1973. No space ships ever have been launched from here but there is an assortment of space hardware on display. The base has been one of the major Houston tourist attractions since it was established.*

P 201   *The zoo now called the Houston Zoological Gardens started in Sam Houston Park in 1902 with one buffalo. The zoo was moved to Hermann Park in 1922.*

P 202   Above left: *The Texas Cyclone is rated one of the best rollercoaster rides in the country. It is one of the features of the Astroworld theme park across the South Loop from the Astrodome complex. The late Roy Hofheinz personally planned and superintended the building of this playground in 1967. He had a genius for design. He was also a compulsive collector and a circus buff. He bought and sold the Ringling Brothers, Barnum, and Bailey show while he was riding high.*
Above right: *The original buildings at Rice were designed by Ralph Adams Cram of the Boston architectural firm of Cram, Goodhue, and Ferguson. The style has been described as Cram's own combination of Byzantine, Romanesque, and Venetian Gothic. The first buildings were completed as classes began in 1912.*
Middle: *The University of Houston Cougars play their home football games under the Dome's plastic roof.*
Below: *There are some others today and some of them are bigger, but the Astrodome was the first air-conditioned baseball stadium in the world. It was completed in 1965.*

P 203   Above: *The well-paid people drawn to the area by the space base have helped make Clear Lake a major yachting center. Traffic gets very heavy on weekends in the channel connecting Clear Lake with Galveston Bay.*
Middle: *The first two terminals at Houston Intercontinental Airport opened in 1969. Two more terminals have been added since.*
Below: *The Harris County Toll Road Authority engineered one of the area's more spectacular highway interchanges in 1990 to connect U.S. 290 and the Sam Houston Tollway. Dairy farms occupied this area before 1950.*

(continued on page 207)

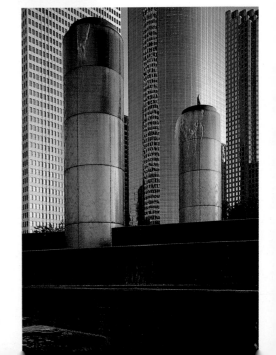

192

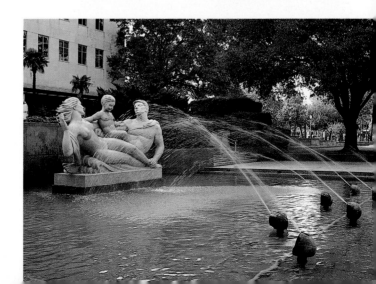

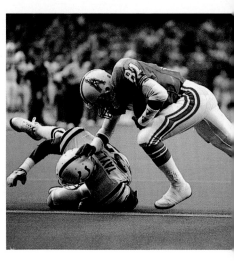

198

202

(continued from page 190)

P 204   Above: The Houston Rockets play their home games in the Summit Arena in Greenway Plaza on the Southwest Freeway.
Below: The Houston Grand Opera and the Houston Ballet got a new home when the Wortham Theater opened on Texas Avenue at the bayou in 1987. The opera and ballet had previously shared Jones Hall with the symphony and the Society for the Performing Arts. Both buildings were built with private funds and contributions but they are owned by the city.

P 205   Above: The close-in suburb of Houston Heights once was a separate town with its own railroad depot. It still retains some of the atmosphere of a small town. Residents emphasized this atmosphere when they celebrated the community's 100th birthday in 1991.
Middle: A new main library building was completed in 1976 across McKinney Street from City Hall. This building was named for the late financier Jesse H. Jones in 1990 after his Houston Endowment contributed $3 million to the library fund.
Below: Several of the original homes still stand in the Heights. Nebraska developers started this community in 1891. It was incorporated in 1896 and annexed to Houston in 1918.

P 206   Above: Houston's link to the sea contributed mightily to the city's growth while cotton and oil fueled the Texas economy.
Middle: The fountain at Fannin and Hermann Drive, nearby, features the Greek columns removed from the original Miller Outdoor Theater when it was remodelled in 1969.
Below: Queen Elizabeth II of England visited Texas in May of 1991 and spent two days seeing the sights and being seen around Houston.

Mayors of Houston

1837	James S. Holman	1886–90	Daniel C. Smith
1838	Francis Moore, Jr.	1890–92	Henry Scheriffus
1839	George W. Lively	1892–96	John T. Browne
1840	Charles Bigelow	1896–98	Horace Baldwin Rice
1841–42	John D. Andrews	1898–1900	Samuel H. Brashear
1843	Francis Moore, Jr.	1901–02	John D. Woolford
1844	Horace Baldwin	1902–04	O. T. Holt
1845	W. W. Swain	1904–05	Andrew L. Jackson
1846	James Bailey	1905–13	Horace Baldwin Rice
1847–48	Benjamin P. Buckner	1913–17	Ben Campbell
1849–52	Francis Moore, Jr.	1917	J. J. Pastoriza
1853–54	Nathan Fuller	1917–18	J. C. Hutcheson, Jr.
1855–56	James H. Stevens	1918–21	A. Earl Amerman
1857	Cornelius Ennis	1921–29	Oscar F. Holcombe
1858	Alexander McGowen	1929–33	Walter E. Monteith
1859	William Harrison King	1933–37	Oscar F. Holcombe
1860	Thomas W. Whitmarsh	1937–39	R. H. Fonville
1861	William J. Hutchins	1939–41	Oscar F. Holcombe
1862	Thomas W. House, Sr.	1941–43	C. A. "Neal" Pickett
1863–65	William Andrews	1943–47	Otis Massey
1866	Horace D. Taylor	1947–52	Oscar Holcombe
1867	Alexander McGowen	1953–55	Roy M. Hofheinz
1868–69	Joseph R. Morris	1956–57	Oscar Holcombe
1870–73	Timothy H. Scanlan	1958–63	Lewis W. Cutrer
1874	James T. D. Wilson	1964–73	Louie Welch
1875–76	I. C. Lord	1974–77	Fred Hofheinz
1877–78	James T. D. Wilson	1978–81	Jim McConn
1879	Andrew J. Burke	1982–91	Kathryn J. Whitmire
1880–85	William R. Baker	1992–	Bob Lanier

County Judges, Harris County

1837–39	A. Briscoe	1883–84	E. P. Hamblen
1840–42	I. N. Moreland	1885–92	W. C. Anders
1843–45	A. P. Thompson	1893–96	John G. Tod
1846–48	W. B. Reeves	1897–98	William N. Shaw
1849–55	Harry H. Allen	1899–1902	E. H. Vasmer
1856–60	Charles Shearn	1903–06	Blake Dupree
1861–62	J. S. Stafford	1907–12	A. E. Amerman
1862–65	T. B. I. Hadley	1913–16	W. H. Ward
1866–66	I. S. Roberts	1917–26	Chester H. Bryan
	(Died in office)	1927–30	Norman Atkinson
1866–68	John Brashear (Removed	1931–32	R. H. Spencer
	by Occupation authorities)	1933–36	W. H. Ward
1869–70	M. N. Brewster (Appointed	1937–46	Roy Hofheinz
	by Occupation authorities)	1947–50	Glenn A. Perry
1871–73	J. W. McDonald	1951–58	Bob Casey
1874–75	Alexander McGowen	1959–74	Bill Elliott
1876–82	C. Anson Jones	1975–	Jon Lindsay

Harris County Representatives, U.S. Congress

1846–49	Timothy Pilsbury, Brazoria	
1849–53	Volney E. Howard, San Antonio	
1853–57	Peter H. Bell, Austin	
1857–59	Guy M. Bryan, Brazoria	
1859–61	Andrew J. Hamilton, Austin	
1861–65	CIVIL WAR *	
1865–70	CONGRESS ACCEPTING NO REPRESENTATIVES FROM FORMER CONFEDERATE STATES **	
1870–73	William T. Clark, Galveston	
1873–75	DeWitt C. Giddings, Brenham	
1875–83	Roger Q. Mills, Corsicana	
1833–93	Charles Stewart, Houston	
1893–97	J. C. Hutcheson, Houston	
1897–1903	T. H. Ball, Houston	
1903–05	John Pinkney, Hempstead	
1905–13	John Moore, Richmond	
1913–21	Joe Eagle, Houston	
1921–33	Dan Garrett, Houston	
1933–37	Joe Eagle, Houston	
1937–66	Albert Thomas, Houston	DISTRICT 8
1959–76	Bob Casey, Houston	DISTRICT 22
1966–67	Lera Thomas, Houston	DISTRICT 8
1967–81	Bob Eckhardt, Houston	DISTRICT 8
1967–71	George Bush, Houston	DISTRICT 7
1971–	Bill Archer, Houston	DISTRICT 7
1973–79	Barbara Jordan, Houston	DISTRICT 18
1976–77	Ron Paul, Lake Jackson	DISTRICT 22
1977–79	Bob Gammage, Houston	DISTRICT 22
1979–85	Ron Paul, Lake Jackson	DISTRICT 22
1979–90	Mickey Leland, Houston	DISTRICT 18
1981–	Jack Fields, Humble	DISTRICT 8
1983–	Mike Andrews, Houston	DISTRICT 25
1982–	Jack Brooks, Beaumont	DISTRICT 9 ***
1985–	Tom DeLay, Sugarland	DISTRICT 22
1990–	Craig Washington, Houston	DISTRICT 18

* REPRESENTED IN CSA CONGRESS BY:
  1861–63   Peter W. Gray
  1863–65   A. M. Branch

** A. M. Branch elected to U.S. House in 1866; House refused to accept him.

*** Jack Brooks actually took District 9 seat in 1953. Boundaries rearranged to include part of southeast Harris County in 1982.

Municipalities Wholly or Partly Within Harris County

	INCORPORATED
Baytown	1948
Bellaire	1947
Bunker Hill	1954
Deer Park	1948
El Lago	1961
Friendswood	1960
Galena Park	1935
Hedwig Village	1954
Houston	1837
Humble	1933
Hunters Creek Village	1954
Jacinto City	1946
Jersey Village	1956
Katy	1945
La Porte	1892
Missouri City	1956
Morgan's Point	1949
Nassau Bay	1970
Pasadena	1928
Pearland	1959
Piney Point	1954
Seabrook	1961
Shoreacres	1949
South Houston	1927
Southside Place	1934
Spring Valley	1954
Stafford	1956
Taylor Lake Village	1961
Tomball	1933
Waller	1947
Webster	1958
West Universtiy Place	1925

School Districts in Harris County

Aldine Independent School District
Alief Independent School District
Channelview Independent School District
Clear Creek Independent School District
Crosby Independent School District
Cypress-Fairbanks Independent School District
Deer Park Independent School District
Galena Park Independent School District
Goose Creek Consolidated Independent School District
Houston Independent School District
Huffman Independent School District
Humble Independent School District
Katy Independent School District
Klein Independent School District
La Porte Independent School District
North Forest Independent School District
Pasadena Independent School District
Pearland Independent School District
Sheldon Independent School District
Spring Independent School District
Spring Branch Independent School District
Stafford Independent School District
Tomball Independent School District
Waller Independent School District

Colleges and Universities in Houston/Harris County

Baylor College of Medicine, 1 Baylor Plaza, Houston 77030
Houston Baptist University, 7502 Fondren, Houston 77074
Houston Community College, 22 Waugh, Houston 77007
Lee College, 511 South Whiting, Baytown 77520
North Harris/Montgomery Community College,
    250 South Sam Houston Parkway, Houston 77060
Rice University, 6100 South Main, Houston 77005
San Jacinto College, 8060 Spencer Highway, Pasadena 77505
South Texas College of Law, 1303 San Jacinto, Houston 77002
Texas Southern University, 3100 Cleburne, Houston 77004
Texas Woman's University, 1130 M. D. Anderson, Houston 77030
University of Houston, 4800 Calhoun, Houston, 77004
University of Houston Downtown, 1 Main, Houston 77002
University of Houston Clear Lake,
    2700 Bay Area Boulevard, Houston 77058
University of St. Thomas, 3812 Montrose, Houston 77006
University of Texas Health Science Center,
    1100 Holcombe, Houston, 77030

Sources

The author has drawn on his own recollections and those of numerous colleagues, and on the archives and collections in the Houston Public Library, and on many published works, including:

Albert Thomas, Late a Representative from Texas, U.S. Government Printing Office.
Architectural Survey, Southwest Center for Urban Research and School of Architecture, Rice University.
"Big Town, Big Money," Editorial Staff, *Houston Business Journal.*
Blood and Money, Thomas Thompson.
But Also Good Business, Walter L. Buenger and Joseph A. Pratt.
Campaign for Major League Baseball in Houston, The, Clark Nealon, Robert Nottebart, Stanley Siegel, and James Tinsley.
Corduroy Road, Wallace Davis.
Decisive Years for Houston, Marvin Hurley.
Eagle, The, Autobiography of Santa Anna, edited by Ann Fears Crawford.
Early Days on the Bayou, Ellen Robbins Red.
From Cannon to Campbell, Mickey Herskowitz.
Grand Huckster, The, Edgar W. Ray.
Handbook of Texas, Texas State Historical Association.
History of the Texas Railroads, A, S. G. Reed.
Houston, A History, David G. McComb.
Houston, A History and Guide, American Guide Series Writers Program, Work Projects Administration.
Houston, Super City of the Southwest, William Shelton and Ann Kennedy.
Houston, the Once and Future City, George Fuermann.
Howard, the Amazing Mr. Hughes, Noah Dietrich and Bob Thomas.
Illustrated 20th Century Deep Water Edition of Houston, Texas, Progressive City of the Empire State, W. W. Dexter.
Jesse H. Jones, the Man and the Statesman, Bascom N. Timmons.
John H. Freeman and His Friends, A Story of the Texas Medical Center and How it Began, N. Don Macon.
Joseph Stephen Cullinan, John O. King.
Last American City, The, Douglas Milburn.
Life and Literary Remains of Sam Houston, William Carey Crane.
Night of Violence, Robert V. Haynes.
Port of Houston, The, Marilyn McAdams Sibley.
Raven, The, Marquis James.
Right Stuff, The, Tom Wolfe.

Texas 1874, Edward King and J. Wells Champney.

Texas, The Country and its Men, L. E. Daniell.

Thumb Nail History of the City of Houston, S. O. Young.

Transportation and Urban Development in Houston, 1830-1980, Peter C. Papademetriou.

True Stories of Old Houston and Houstonians, S. O. Young.

Two Thousand Miles in Texas on Horseback, N. A. Taylor.

Visit to Texas in 1831, (author unknown).

William Bollaert's Texas, edited by W. Eugene Hallon and Ruth Lapham Butler.

William Marsh Rice and His Institute, Andrew Forest Muir.

Yellow Rose of Texas, The, Martha Ann Turner.

Index

A

ABC TV Network, 171
Abzug, Bella, 162
Adams, Bud, 132, 137, 144, 189
Adair, Christia, 178, **178**
Abercrombie, J. S., 72, 104
Addicks Reservoir, 86
Aedes Aegypti mosquito, 34
A. H. Belo Co., 109
Air conditioning boom, 109
Air France, 138, 166
Air pollution, 146
Airmail, first, 77
Alamo, 3, 4, 8
Albert Thomas Convention Center, 146, 148, **148**, 161
Aldrin, Buzz, 139, **139**
Ali, Mohammed, 60, **60**
Allen, Augustus C., 3, 4, **5**, 6, 10
Allen, Charlotte, 10, 12, **12**
Allen, John Kirby, 3, 4, **5**, 6, 10
Allen Center, 152, **152**, 163, 166
Allen Parkway Village, 90, 95, **95**
Allen's Landing, 65, **65**, 183
Allied Bank Tower, 165, 166
Alley Theater, 103, 106, 149, **149**, 161
American Bar Association, 140

American Football League, 132
American General Center, 134, 166, 189
American General Co., 134, 166, 189
American League, 137
American Republics Oil Co., 61
Amtrak, 153
Amtrak Station, 50, 157
Anderson, Frank, 61
Anderson, M. D., 61, 62, 87, 95, **95**
Anderson Clayton Co., 61, 72, 87, 126
Andrews, Mike, 169, 184, **184**
Annexation, 1948, 102
  1956, 103
Annexation Wars, 120
Annunciation Catholic Church, 19, **19**
Antioch Baptist Church, 152, **152**
Arboretum, **74**, 75
Archer, Bill, 149
Argovitz, Jerry, 170
Arkla, 154
Armco Steel, 94
Armed Forces Induction Center, 60
Armstrong, Neil, 137, 139
Astrodomain, 147
Astrodome, 131, 143, 144, 161, 168, 170, 181, 189, 190, **202**
  opening of, 144

Astronauts, **126**, 127, 138
Astroworld Park, 147, 168, 190, **202**
Auditorium Hotel, 172, **172**
Audubon, John James, 8
Austin, 16
Austin, John, 3, 6
Austin, Moses, 3
Austin, Stephen F., 3, 4, **5**, 13
Automobiles, first, 51

B
Bagby, T. M., 23
Bailey, W. H., 39
Baker and Botts, 58
Baker, James A., 57
Baker, James A., III, 58
Baker, W. R., 39
Baldwin, W. W., 53
Ball, Tom, 41, 70, 71
Bank of the Southwest, 126, 172, 175
Bank One, 175
Bank rescue, 80
Bankers' Trust, 53
Barbara Jordan High School, 178, **179**
Barbirolli, John, 58
Barker Reservoir, 86
Baseball Museum, 77
Basilian Fathers, 103, 105
Bates, W. B., 87
Battle of San Jacinto, 6, 7, 12
Battlestein, Philip, 120, 147
Battlestein's, 120, 147
Baylor College of Medicine, **96**, 97, 98, 106
Baylor University, 99
Bayou Bend Museum, 70, **71**
"Bayou City", 3
Bayou City Guards, 23
Bayou Club, 182, **182**
Baytown Tunnel, 103
Bellaire, 53
Benda, Ilona, 67, 71
Bennett, Archie, 131, **131**
Ben Taub Hospital, 139, 178
Bentsen, Lloyd, 184, **184**
Bertner, E. W., 88
Beth Israel, 24
Biggers, John, 178
Big Inch Pipeline, 94

Binion, Jack, 115
Binz Building, 40, **41**, 44
Binz, Jacob, 40, 44
Blaffer, R. L., 62
Blockade runners, 20
Blood and Money, 73
Bollaert, William, 17
Bonham, Don, 144, **144**
Borden, Gail, 6, 10, 16
Borden, Thomas, 16
Bourdon, Ed, 78
Braniff Airways, 87, 90, **90**
Bremond, Margaret, 18
Bremond, Paul, 18
Brinkley, David, 128
Briscoe, A. C., 10, 14
British Caledonian Airways, 163
Brooks, Jack, 184, **184**
Brown and Root, 86, 109, 136, 171, **171**, 189
Brown Foundation, 145
Brown, George R., 78, 84, 104, 109, 114, 136, 166, 169, **169**, 190
Brown, Herman, 84, 104, 171
Brown, Lee, 164, **165**, 167
Brown Shipbuilding Co., 98, **98**
Buccaneer Hotel, 68
Buff Stadium, 77
Buffalo Bayou, 6, 86
Buffalo Bayou, Brazos and Colorado, 18
Buffalo Bayou Co., 14, 16
Buffalo Bayou Ship Channel Co., 23, 28
Building permits record, 166, 167
Burke, Jackie, 120, **121**
Burke Baker Planetarium, 188
Burlington streamliner, **88**, 89
Busses, first, 74
Bush, George, 122, **122**, 129, 146, 149, 168, 179
Bush Presidential Library, 179
Butler, George, 104

C
C and I Life Building, 167
Cable TV franchises, 156, 163
Calkins, Bernard, 136
Cameron, H. S., 72
Camp Logan, 63, 67, **67**, 72
riot, 63, 64, 67

Camp Logan hospital, 139
Capital National Plaza, 165
Capitol Cities Co., 109, 171
Capitol Hotel, 13, 34, **35**, 57
Carlton, L. A., 62
Carnegie, Andrew, 50
Carnegie Library, 50, **50**
Carry Nation Saloon, 52, **53**
Carter, O. M., 43
Carter Field, 87
Casey, Bob, 129, 162
Castillo, Leonel, 150
Catholic church, first, 16
Census of 1850, 18
Census of 1860, 20
Census of 1870, 24
Census of 1880, 33
Census of 1890, 41
Census of 1900, 49
Census of 1910, 53
Census of 1920, 66
Census of 1930, 78
Census of 1940, 88
Census of 1950, 109
Census of 1960, 132
Census of 1970, 149
Census of 1980, 165
Census of 1990, 177, 185
Center for the Retarded, 150
Central High School, 82, **82**
Central Library Building, 77
Challenger (spacecraft), 171
Champions Golf Club, 120, **121**
Cheek and Neal Co., 69
Chemical Bank, 172
Chevron Tower, 166, **166**
Christ Church Cathedral, 19, **19**
Chronicle, 37
Chu, Paul, 172
Cities Service, 125
Citizens' Electric Light & Power Co., 34
City Bank of Houston, 24
City Charter Election, 1955, 114, 115
City Council, expanded, 164
City Election, 1955, 116
City Hall, Market Square, 135, 117, **117**
City Hall Cafeteria, 123
City Hall and Opera House, 27
City Library, 161, **205**, 207

City Partnership Limited, 170
City Planning Commission, 186
City Planning and Zoning Commission, 186
Clark, Beverly, 177
Clark, R. Lee, 99
Clayton, Ben, 62
Clayton, Nicholas, 19, 21
Clayton, Susan, 122, 136
Clayton, Will, 62, 66, 122, 146
Clayton home, 122, **123**
Clayton Homes, 136
Clear Lake City, 136
    annexation, 163
Clements, Bill, 168
Clinton, 29, 32, **32**, 43
Clopper's Bar, 18
Coastal Subsidence District, 162
Cohen, Raymond, 104
Coke, Richard, 27
Colleges and universities, 213
Collingworth, James, 12
Columbia, 7
Commercial National Bank, 39
Community Chest, 66
Congress Square, 10
Congressmen, 209
Connally, Ben, 123
Connally, John, 173
Connally, Nellie, 173
Continental Airlines, 170
Continental League, 137
Continental Oil, 112
Contraflow lanes, 163
County judges, 209
Convention Hall, 79, **79**
Cooley, Denton, 150, **150**
Cork Club, 111
Cotton compress, first, 17
Cotton exports, **26**, 27, 76, **76**
Courthouse Oak, 148, **148**
Courtland Place, 150, **151**
Cousins, R. B., 74
Cox, Archibald, 140, 156
Cram, Ralph Adams, 190
Cram, Goodhue, and Ferguson, 190
Crockett, Davy, 3
Croneis, Carey, 127, **127**
Cronkite, Walter, 155

Crow, Trammell, 149
Crowley, Eileen T., 174
Cruger, Jacob, 16
Cryer, Sherwood, 179
Cullen, Hugh Roy, 73, 103, 111
Cullen, Lillie, 73, 103
Cullen Center, 132-134, 152
Cullen Foundation, 103
Cullen house, **72**, 73
Cullen Sculpture Garden, 174, **174**
Cullinan, Craig, Jr., 137
Cullinan, Joseph S., 51, **54**, 55, 61, 62, 77
Cullinan, Nina, 104
Cultural Arts Council of Houston, 186
Cutrer, Lewis, 124

D
Dallas Cowboys, 132
Daniel, Alfred, 74
Daughters of the Republic of Texas, 49
Daum, David, 126
Davis, Edmund J., 23, 27
Davis, Jefferson, 29
Davis, Morgan, 136
Dean, Dizzy, 77
DeBakey, Michael, 106
Deep Water Jubilee, 58
DeHartog, Jan, 140
Demeret, Jimmy, 120, **121**
Democratic National Convention,
     1928, 38, 77
DeMoss, Hal, 169
Deneau, Paul, 155
Denson, Franklin, 175
Desegregation, 121-124
Diana (ship), 39
Dibble, Elias, 152
Dick Dowling statue, 30, **30**
Dickson Gun Plant, 94
Dietrich, Noah, 64
Dillard's, 135, 172
Dingwall, James C., 103
Dixie automobile, 77
Dowling, Dick, 23
Dreamliners, 136
Duddleston, Wayne, 153
Dun and Bradstreet, 109
Duncan Coffee Co., 69
Dyer, Dallas, 111

E
Eagle (spacecraft), 137, 148
Eastern Airlines, 87
Eckhart, Bob, 146
Economic Development Council, 174
Economic Summit, 179
Edy, John North, 98
Ehlers, H. J., 104
801 Travis, 165
Electric street cars, 40, **40**
Elkins, James A., 62, 66
Ellington, Eric, 63
Ellington Field, 63, **66**, 67, 90, 170
Elysian Overpass, 116
Emancipation Park, 152
Emerald Room, 107
Emmott, Catherine, 67, 71
Enco, 154
Enron, 170
Entex, 154
Environmental Protection Agency, 164
Epsom Downs, 85
Equal Rights Amendment, 162
Eschenbach, Cristoph, 58
Ethyl Corp., 112
Eversole, Jerry, 179
Exxon, 44, 154
Exxon Building, 75

F
Fallbrook National Bank, 174, **175**
Farish, W. S., 62
Farm Road 1960 (FM 1960), 120
Farmers' Cooperative Market, 117, **117**
Fashion, Ben Wolfman's, 125
Federal Building, 134
Ferber, Edna, 107
Ferguson, Jim, 52
Fiesta Stores, 144, **144**
Fifth Ward, 17
Finn, Alfred, 86
Finger's Furniture Stores, 77
Finlay, Carlos, 34
Fire Department ambulances, 158
Fire Department Central Station, 50, **51**
Fire Department Museum, 159, **159**
First Baptist Church, 16
First City National Bank, 62, 172
First City National Bank Building, 132

First City Tower, 165
First International Bank Tower, 162
First Methodist Church, 16
First National Bank, 23
First Presbyterian Church, 16
First Republic Bank, 173
First Ward, 17
Flaherty, Pat, 110, **111**
Flood of 1935, 86
Foley, W. L., home, 21, **21**
Foley Brothers, 21, 103
Foley's, 106, **107**, 110, 124, 136
Fondren, W. W., 62, 66
Fondren home, 150, **151**
Fonteno, Jim, 179
Ford assembly plant, 69, **69**
Ford Foundation, 149
Ford Motor Credit Co., 168
Foreman, Percy, 173, 174, 176, **177**
Foster, Marcellus E., 39
Founder's Cemetery, 4, **5**
Four Allen Center, 168
Four Seasons Hotel, 168
Fourth Ward, 17, 150
Foyt, A. J., 145, **145**
Frank, Rueven, 161
Freedman, Jakie, 107
Freedmantown, 23
Freeman, John, 87, 88
Frost Brothers, 147
Fuermann, George, 66
Fulbright, Crooker, Freeman and Bates, 156

G
Gable, Clark, 79
Gable Street Light Plant, 34, **35**
Galleria, 125, 133, 134, 149, 188, **192**
    site, **134**, 135
Galveston, 18, 23
Galveston, Battle of, 23
Galveston, Port of, 24, 28, 41, 94, 181
Galveston-Houston Corp., 49, 136
Gambling, 106, 107
Gas lights, 23
G. E. Credit, 168
Geizendanner, Charlie, 111
General Sherman (locomotive), **26**, 27
Gentry Volunteers, 23

George R. Brown Convention Center, 148, 170, 190, **200**
Getty Oil Co., 170
Giant (novel), 109
Gilley, Mickey, 179
Gilley's, 179
Gilruth, Robert, 137, **137**
Glen, John K., 104
Glenn, John, 138
Glenwood Cemetery, 13, **13**, 168
Goddard, C. B., 62
Goldberg, Billy, 153
Goodyear blimp, 189, **200**
Goyen, Johnny, 131, **131**
Grain elevator, first, 29
Gramm, Phil, 184, **184**
Grand Central Station, 49, 50, **51**
Grant's, 123
Gray, Bob, 110, **110**
Grayson, Peter W., 12
Great Depression, 80
Great Southern Insurance Co., 53
Greater Houston Chamber of Commerce, 174
Greater Houston Partnership, 174
Greenway Plaza, 132, **132**, 134, 161, 207
Greenwood, Jim, 186
Greer, David, 104
Griffin, Charles, 23
Groesbeeck, Abraham, 13
Gulf Building, 77
Gulf Coast Waste Disposal Authority, 149
Gulf, Colorado, and Santa Fe, 24
Gulf Freeway, 98, 103
Gulfgate, 120, **120**, 126
Gulf Oil, 112
Gulf Tower, 166, **166**

H
Hackney, Clint, 169
Hall, Anthony, 165
Halliburton, 171
Hardy Street Toll Road, 170
Harris County, 6
Harris County Commissioners Court, 170, 179
Harris County Courthouse, 11
Harris County Domed Stadium, 131, **202**

Harris County Heritage Society, 15, **15**, 25
    44, 117, 129, 169
Harris County Hospital District, 140, 178
Harris County Jail, 183
Harris County Park Board, 129
Harris County Republican Party, 129
Harris County Toll Road Authority,
    170, 190
Harris, Jack, 111
Harris, John Richardson, 11
Harrisburg, 4, 6, 11, 14, 15, 16
    annexation, 77
Harrisburg County, 11
Hart Galleries, 173
Hartung, Christin, 165
Hawkins, G. W., 51
Haynes, Richard "Racehorse," 176, **177**
Heard, Jack, 107, 167
Hearst Corp., 171
Henke, Henry, 119
Henke Building, **118**, 119
Heritage Plaza, 173
Herman Brown Park, 145, **145**
Hermann, George, 55, 61, 63, **63**, 93, 189
Hermann Hospital, 61, 63, **63**, 99
Hermann Park, 61, 99, 130, **130**, 189,
    190, **197**, **199**, **201**
Hermann Park Zoo, 175
Hill, Joan Robinson, 73
Hill, John, 73
Hill house, **72**, 73
Hilton, Conrad, 89, 125
Hilton Hotels, 125
Hines, Gerald, 133, **133**, 134, 135, 146,
    149, 160, 166, 167, 188, **192**
Hinton, W. H., 131
Hitchcock, 94
Hobby, Oveta Culp, 153
Hobby, William P., 37, 153
Hobby, W. P., Jr., 153
Hobby Airport, 135, 139, **139**, 150
Hofheinz, Fred, 156, 175
Hofheinz, Roy, 78, 109, 114, 116, 124,
    128, 131, **131**, 137, 138, 143, 144,
    145, 148, 169, 181, 190
Hofheinz-City Council Battle, 114,
    115, 116
Hogg, Ima, 70, 161

Hogg, James Stephen, 70
Hogg, Mike, 67, 70, 71
Hogg, Will, 67, 70, 71, 78
Holcombe, Oscar F., 53, 68, **68**, 71, 83,
    97, 103, 104, 112, 114, 116, 125, 155
Holcombe home, 97, **97**
Hollis, John, 145
Hoover, Herbert, 79, 81
Horowitz, Will, 181
House, Edward M., 20
House, T. W., 20, **26**, 27
House, T. W., III, 70, 71
Houston, Sam, 4, 6, 7, 8, **9**, 10, 12, 13,
    16, 20, 22, 56
Houston, 6, 7, 16
Houston Aeros, 155
Houston and Texas Central Railroad, 20,
    27, 49
Houston Artillery, 23
Houston Art League, 62
Houston Astros, 143, 165, 173, 189, **198**
Houston Ballet, 146, 207
Houston Baptist College/University, 131
Houston Bar Association, 176
Houston Board of Trade and Cotton
    Exchange, 28
Houston Buffs, 137
Houston Business League, 44
Houston Center, 150, 156, 162, 163,
    166, 175
Houston Chamber of Commerce, 44, 99,
    115, 124, 156, 174
Houston Chronicle, 39, 59, 71, 145, 171
Houston Chronicle and Herald, 39
Houston Chronicle Building, 16
Houston City Council expansion proposal,
    185
Houston City Hall, 88, 93, **93**
Houston City Street Railway Co., 43
Houston College for Negroes, 121
Houston Colt .45s, 143
Houston Community College, 153, **154**,
    155
Houston Cotton Exchange and Board
    of Trade, 28
Houston Cotton Exchange Building, 33,
    33
Houston Country Club, 52, 104, 120

222

Houston Electric Light and Power Co., 34
Houston Endowment, Inc., 126, 134, 149, 171, 207
Houston Fat Stock Show and Rodeo, 79, 83, 111
Houston-Galveston Interurban, 56, 58, 59
Houston Gamblers, 170
Houston Gas and Fuel Co., 23, 77
Houston Gas Light Co., 34
Houston Golf Club, 52
Houston Grand Opera, 125, 146, 207
Houston Gulf Gas Co., 77
Houston Heights, 43, 205, 207
  annexation, 62
Houston Herald, 39
Houston High School, 82
Houston Horse Show Association, 104
Houston House, 143
Houston Independent School District, 86, 111, 112, 153, 167
Houston Intercontinental Airport, 134, 135, 148, 180, 181, 190, 203
Houston International Airport, 129
Houston International Festival, 186, 186
Houston Light Guard, 28, 29
Houston Light Guard Armory, 32, 32
Houston Lighting and Power Co., 34
Houston Livestock Show and Rodeo, 161
Houston Lyceum and Carnegie Library, 49
Houston Magazine, 165
Houston Municipal Airport, 87, 90
Houston Museum of Natural Science, 130, 130, 188, 196
Houston National Bank, 39, 80, 81
Houston National Exchange Bank, 39
Houston Natural Gas Co., 74, 154, 170
Houston Navigation Co., 18
Houston Negro Hospital, 77
Houston Oilers, 132, 144, 145, 189, 198
Houston, original port of, 64, 65
Houston Pipeline Co., 74
Houston Polo Club, 182
Houston, Port of, 24, 24, 94, 178, 181
Houston Post, 37, 66, 145, 171
Houston Post Dispatch, 37, 74
Houston Press, 39, 59, 59
Houston Public School Art League, 62
Houston Rockets, 161, 204, 207
Houston School Board, 122, 178, 181

Houston School District, 74
Houston Ship Channel, 24, 34, 54, 155, 206, 207
  deepening of, 103, 129
Houston Sports Association, 131, 161, 168, 189
Houston State Fair, 29
Houston Symphony Orchestra, 58, 146
Houston Telegraph, 16
Houston World Trade Council, 174
Houston Zoological Gardens, 190, 201
Howard, The Amazing Mr. Hughes (book), 64
Hughes, Howard R., 49, 64
Hughes, Howard R., Jr., 49, 87, 90, 90, 91, 162
Hughes home, 92, 93
Hughes Tool Co., 49, 94
Humason, Granville, 72
Humble Building, 75, 75, 77
Humble Co., 44, 75, 129, 132, 136
Humble/Exxon Building, 124, 124
Humble Oil Field, 48, 49
Humble Oil and Refining Co., 62
Hunt, Caroline, 168
Hunt, Lamar, 132
Huntley, Chet, 128
Hurricane Carla, 136
Hurricane of 1900, 41
Hutcheson, J. C., 41
Hyatt Regency Hotel, 153

I
Ideson, Julia, 49
Incarnate Word Academy, 21, 21
International Harmon Trophy, 87
InterNorth, 170

J
Jack Rabbit Road, 120
Jackson, Andrew, 4
Jackson, Dick, 104
James, Marquis, 7
Jarriel, Tom, 137, 142, 142
Jaworski, Leon, 140, 140, 156, 157
Jefferson Davis Hospital, 29, 29, 139, 179
Jeppeson Stadium, 132
Jesse Jones toll bridge, 167
Jetero Corp., 125

"Jim Crow" laws, 121
JMB-Houston Center Partners, 175
Johnson, Lyndon B., 80, **81**, 136, 142
Johnson, Philip, 3, 135, 160, 188, **192**
Johnson, President, and Mrs., 131, **131**
Johnston, Ralph, 134
Jones, Jesse H., 39, 43, **43**, 44, 53, 57, 62,
  77, 78, 80, 81, 86, **92**, 116, 126,
  158, 207
Jones, John T., 109
Jones, Tilford, 86
Jones Hall, 146, 159, 161, 207
Jones Lumber Co., 44
Jones Plaza, 161
Jordan, Barbara, 123, 126, **126**, 146, 175
Josey, J. E., 37
Joske's, 106, 135, 149, 172
Journal (newspaper), 37

K
Keeland, J. W., 62
Kellum, Nathaniel, 117
Kellum-Noble house, **116**, 117, 129
Kennedy, John, 127, **127**, 136
Kirkland, Bill, 129
Kern, Buster, 107
KGUL TV, Channel 11, 109, 112
KHOU TV, Channel 11, 109, 112, **113**
KHTV, Channel 39, 147
Kiam Building, 40, **40**
Kiepper, Alan, 167, 177
Kirby, John Henry, 38, **38**, 43
Kirby Building, 125
Kirby Lumber Co., 38
Kirby Mansion, 38, **39**
Kirby Petroleum Co., 38
Kirksey, George, 137
KLEE TV, Channel 2, 108, 109
Klevenhagen, Johnny, 183
KNUZ TV, Channel 39, 112
KPRC Radio, 74, 109
KPRC TV, Channel 2, 108, 109, 114, **114**
Kraft, Christopher, 137, **137**
KRIV TV, Channel 26, 153
KTRH Radio, 78
KTRK TV, Channel 13, 109, 112,
  113, 171
KTXH TV, Channel 20, 167
KUHT TV, Channel 8, 112, **113**

Ku Klux Klan, 71
KXYZ Radio, 86

L
Labor State Bank, 81
La Carafe, **118**, 119
Lake Conroe, 149
Lake Houston, 112
Lake Livingston, 142
Lamar, Mirabeau, 12, 15, **15**
Lamar Hotel, 77, 86, 166, 167, **167**,
  168, 169
Lamar Hotel Suite 8-F, 114, 125
Lamour, Dorothy, 107
Lancaster Hotel, 172, **172**
Lanier, Bob, 168, 173, 175, 177, 184, 185
Laura (ship), 8
Laurenzo, Ninfa, 144, **144**
Lawson, Bill, 123
Lay, Kenneth, 170
Lee, Albert, 109
Lee, El Franco, 179
Lee, Sheila Jackson, 177
Lee, T. P., 105
Leland, Mickey, 123, 175, 181
LeRoy, Moses, 164
Levine, Max, 124
Levy, Abe and Leo, 128
Levy Brothers, 128, 129
LH7 Ranch, 79, **79**
Library, 161, **205**, 207
Liedtke, Hugh, 142
Link, J. W., 103, 105
Lincoln, Abraham, 20
Lindsay, Jon, 170, 179, 184, **184**
Little Inch Pipeline, 94
Liquor-by-the-drink legalized, 161
Lockett, Reese, 111
Loew's State Theater, 82, **82**, 166, 167
Longcope, C. S., 28
Long Reach Terminal, 72, 125
Loop 610, 138
Lorenzo, Frank, 170
Lovett, Martha, 104
Lovett, R. S., 45
Lovett home, 45, **45**
Lumbermen's National Bank, 53
Lunar and Planetary Institute, 129, **129**
Lutheran church, first, 20

Lynch, Nathaniel, 7
Lynch's Ferry, 7
Lynchburg, 6
Lynchburg Ferry, 7, **7**
Lyndon B. Johnson Hospital, 178
Lyndon B. Johnson Manned Spacecraft
    Center, 156, 190, **200**
Lyndon B. Johnson School of Public
    Affairs, 126
Lyons, E. A. "Squatty," 179
Lyric Theater, 166

M
Magnolia Brewery, 42, **42**
Magnolia Park annexed, 77
Magruder, John B., 23
Main Building, 77
Main Post Office, 134
Majestic Metro, 181, **181**
Mancuso, Gus, 77
M & M Building, 183, **183**
Mann, Pamelia, 11, 12, 119
Manned Spacecraft Center, 136, 190,
    200
Mansion House, 12, 119
Market Square, 10, 125
Market Square Historic District, 170
Marine Banking and Trust Co., 81
Marine State Bank, 81
Marks, Emil, 79, 111
Marks, Maudeen, 111
Marshall Plan, 146
Martin, Pepper, 77
Maryland Club Coffee, 69
Massey, Otis, 95-98
Maxwell House Coffee plant, 69, **69**
Mayors of Houston, 208
MBank, 172, 175
McCarthy, Glenn H., 85, 102, **102**, 105,
    107, 109, 125, 174
McCarthy, Joe, 109
McCarthy Oil and Gas Corp., 102
McCasland, Barney, 115, **115**, 125
McConn, Jim, 163, 167, 177
McConnell, J. R., 171
McCormick, Peggy, 49
McDonald's, 45
McGowen, Alexander, 23
McGowen, Ernest, 165

McKissick, Jeff, 158
Mcmullen, John, 168
M. D. Anderson Foundation, 98
M. D. Anderson Hospital, 95, **95**, 99,
    189, **196**
Mecom, John, 130, 138, 145, 188
Mecom, John, Jr., 175
Mecom Fountain, 188, **193**
Media News Group, 171
Medwick, Ducky, 77
Memorial Drive, 116, 120, 188, **193**
Memorial Golf Course, 87, 189, **199**
Memorial Hospital, 150, 162
Memorial Park, 7, 67, **74**, 75, 189, **199**
Memorial Professional Building, 165
Mendenhall, O. C., 144, **144**
Menil Collection, 172, **172**
Menil, Dominique de, 153, 172
Menil, John de, 153, 172, 173
Mercantile Bank, 172
Meridian Hotel, 166
Methodist Hospital, 66, 106, 111, 189,
    199
Metro, 167
Metropolitan Life Insurance Co., 149
Metropolitan Theater, 82, **82**, 166, 167
Metropolitan Transit Authority, 156, 163
Metro rail plans, 169, 173, 177, 185
Mewhinney, Hubert, 186
Meyer, Leopold, 66, 104
Michigan State Employees Pension
    System, 173
Milburn, Douglas, 3
Miller, Jesse, 147
Miller, Ray, 110, **110**
Miller Theater, 147, 207
Minute Women, 111
Mission Control Center, 137, **137**
Missouri City, 128
Missouri, Kansas, and Texas, 27
Mitchell, A. L., 104
Mitchell, George, 153
Mobil Oil, 112
Moody, D. M., 64
Moody, W. L., III, 80
Moore, Francis, 16
Morgan, Charles, 28, 43
Morgan, Emily, 6
Morgan, James, 6

225

Morgan City, 28
Morgan Line, 28, 32
Morgan's Point, 4, 27, 29, 43
Morris, Joseph, 23
Mosbacher, Robert, 177
"Mr. Million," 125
Municipal Airport, 112
Municipalities in Harris County, 211
Murchison, Clint, 132
Museum of Fine Arts, **54**, 55, 62, 70, 174
Music Hall, 116
Mutscher, Gus, 153

N

N.A.A.C.P., 178
NASA Visitors Center, 184
Nassau Bay Motor Inn, 128, **128**
Nation, Carry, 52, **53**
National Aeronautics and Space
    Administration, 127, 136
National Association of Broadcasters, 141,
    157
National Association of Homebuilders, 148
National Bank of Commerce, 80, 81
National Bankers' Life Insurance Co., 150
National City Lines, 146
National Endowment for the Arts, 186
National Football League, 132, 145
National Hockey League, 155
National Register of Historic Places, 170
National Women's Conference, 162
National League, 137
Navigation District, 54, 148
NCNB Corp., 173
Neils Esperson Building, 77
Neiman-Marcus Co., 125
New Kentucky, 6
Newman, Barnett, 153
New Washington, 6
Nichols, Ebenezer, 18
Ninfa's, 144
Nixon, Richard, 140, 141, **141**, 142, 156,
    157, 159, 161
Norsworthy, Oscar, 66

O

Oakes, Roy, 150
O'Brien, Pat, 105
O'Connor, Ralph, 153

Odd Fellows Hall, 16
Offshore Oil Rig development, 104
Oil price collapse, 169, 170
Olshan, Immanuel, 164
Olshan's, 164, **164**
Omaha and South Texas Land Co., 43
One Houston Center Building, 162
One Shell Plaza, 135, **135**, 146
Optimists' Club, 76
Orange Show, 158, **158**
Oscar F. Holcombe Civic Center, 161
Oshman, Jake, 129
Oshman's, 128, 129

P

Panhandle Eastern, 175
Panic of 1873, 27
Pardee, Jack, 170
Park and Ride, 163
Pasadena, 120
Patton, H. L., "Pat," 175
Paul, Ron, 162
Paved street, first, 36, **36**
Pei, I. M., 160
Pelli, Cesar, 183
Pennzoil, 135, 142, 143, 170, 171
Pennzoil Place, 135, 137, **137**, 153
Peoples' State Bank, 81
Perfecto dry cleaning plant, 52, **52**
Petrochemical development 103
Petroleum Club, 124
Petroleum Refining Co., 61
Petruzielo, Frank, 181
Phillips explosion, 175
Pickett, C. A. Neal, 177
Pillot, Eugene, 38
Pillot Building, 38, **38**, 170
Pin Oak Stables, 104
Plaza del Oro, 149
Polio, 112
Port of Houston, 156, **157**
    tours, 156
Port of Houston Authority, 56
Potter, Hugh, 70, 71
Previn, Andre, 58
Prince, Doug, 85
Prince's Drive-Ins, **84**, 85
Prince Phillip, 168
Produce Terminal, 125

Prohibition, 64
Prudential Insurance, 112, 189
Public National Bank, 80, 81
Public schools, establishment, 29

Q
Quebedeaux, Walter, 112, 115, **115**
Queen Elizabeth, 168, **206**, 207

R
Radack, Steve, 179
Railroads (before Civil War), 20
Ranger automobile, 69, **69**, 77
Rather, Dan, 137, 142, 159, 161
Raymond, Joan, 171, 176, **176**, 181
Reagan, Billy, 171, 176
Reconstruction, 23
Reconstruction Era indebtedness, 39
Reconstruction Finance Corp., 81, 93
Red Cross, 139
Reed, Clarence, 72
Reed, Walter, 34
Reed Roller Bit Co., 72
Redfish Reef, 18
Remington Hotel, 168
Republic Bank, 160, **160**, 166
Republic of Texas, 7, 10
Republic Tower, 161, **161**
Republican National Committee, 179
Republican National Convention, 1992, 179-181
Reyes, Ben, 165
Rice, H. Baldwin, 52
Rice, William Marsh, 13, 17, **17**, 18, 20, 34, 52
Rice, William Marsh II, 52
Rice home, 25, **25**
Rice Hotel, 34, **35**, 57, **62**, 63, 140, 158, **158**
Rice Institute, 57
Rice University, 57, 129, 131, 134, 136, 179, 189, 190, **197, 202**
    campus, 60, **61**
    stadium, 109, 144, 189, **197**
Rickey, Branch, 137
Ritz-Carlton Hotel, 168
Ritz Theater, 181, **181**
River Oaks Country Club, 70, **70**
River Oaks Shopping Center, 73, **73**

River Oaks Subdivision, 71
Riverside General Hospital, 77
Riverside Terrace, **146**, 147
Robinson, Ash, 73
Robinson, Judson, 165
Rolla (ship), 7
Roosevelt, Franklin, 78, 79, 81, 92, 93
Root, Dan, 84
Ross, Delores, 123
Rothko, Mark, 153
Rothko Chapel, 153
Royal Dutch Airline, KLM, 128
Ryan, Nolan, 165, 173
S
Sabine Pass, Battle of, 23
St. Joseph's Hospital, 36, **36**
St. Louis Cardinals, 77
St. Luke's Episcopal Hospital, 99, 150
St. Luke's Medical Tower, 183, **183**
Sakowitz, Bernard, 178
Sakowitz, Robert, 178
Sakowitz, Simon, 178
Sakowitz, Tobias, 178
Sakowitz, 40, 135, **135**, 149, 178
Salant, Dick, 161
Salk, Jonas, 112
Salmon, George, 104
Salt Grass Trail Ride, 110, 111
Sam Houston (ship), 156, **156**
Sam Houston Coliseum, 83, 88, 111, 116, 127, 140, 155, 161
Sam Houston High School, 80, 82, **82**
Sam Houston Park, 25, **25**, 42, **42**, 44, 117, 129, 188, 190, **191, 192, 193**
Sam Houston Race Park Limited, 181
Sam Houston Tollway, 170, 190, **203**
Sam Houston Zephyr (train), 87
San Antonio, 16
San Diego Rockets, 153
San Felipe, 6
San Felipe Courts, 90
San Jacinto Battleground, 6, 49
San Jacinto Battleground State Park, 8, **9**
San Jacinto High School, 86
San Jacinto Monument, 86, **86**, 88
San Jacinto Ordnance Depot, 129
Santa Anna, Antonio Lopez de, 3, 4, 6, 8, **9**
Sartwelle, J. W., 83

Satilla (ship), 61, 65, **65**
Sawmill, first, 17
Scanlan, T. H., 23, 27, 31, **31**, 56
Scanlan Building, 56, **56**
Scanlan home, **44**, 45, 188
Scanlan sisters, 181
Schindler, Raymond, 153
Schnitzer, Kenneth, 132, 133, **133**, 134, 155, 161
School Board, expanded, 167
School districts in Harris County, 212
Schrimpf Alley, 136
Scripps, E. W., 39, 59
Scripps-Howard, 59
Seagraves, Odie, 80
Secession Convention of 1861, 20
Secession vote, 20
Second National Bank, 126
Second Ward, 17
Securities Exchange Commission, 150
Segregation, 121-124
Settegast, Julius, 86
Shadyside, 55, **55**
Shamrock Hotel, 105, 107, 111, 125, 172, 174, 176, **176**, 188
   opening, 107
Sharp, Frank, 125, 127, 128, 131, 150, 153
Sharp, Walter, 49
Sharp-Hughes Tool Co., 49
Sharpstown Center, 125, **125**, 128, 136
Sharpstown Country Club, 166
Sharpstown State Bank, 125, **125**
Sheffield Steel, 94
Shell Oil, 146, 148, 149
Shell Plaza, One and Two, 149
Shell Refinery, 77
Shepherd, B. A., 23
Sheraton-Lincoln Building, 134
Siff, Iris, 149
Sinclair, 61
Singleton, Dean, 171
Sisters of Charity of the Incarnate Word, 34, 39
1600 Smith Building, 168
610 Loop, channel bridge, 155, **155**, 156
Sixth Ward, 17
Smith, Al, 78, 79
Smith, Ashbel, 8
Smith, Ben Fort, 11

Smith, Carl, 169
Smith, D. C., 39
Smith, R. E. Bob, 137, 143, 144
Smith Street, 162, **162**
Sources, 214, 215
Southern Motors Manufacturing Association, 69, 77
Southern Pacific, 32, 39, 43
Southern Pacific Building, 68, **68**
Southern Pacific Hospital, 56, **57**
Southern Pacific Station, 157
Southern Steamship Co., 58
South Main Baptist Church, 52
South Penn Oil Co., 143
South Texas National Bank, 39
Southwest Airlines, 139, 150
Southwest Freeway, 128, 131
Space City, 138
Spanish-American War, 28
Spindletop, 49
Stafford, 20
Stage lines, 17
Staub, John, 73
Sterling, Frank, 62
Sterling, Ross, 37, 62, 75, **75**, 80
Sterling bay house, 76, **76**
Sterling Oil Co., 75
Stokowski, Leopold, 58
Stone and Webster, 49
Stop signs, first, 66
Storer Cable Co., 163
Sugarland, 24
Summit Arena, 161, **204**, 207
Sunray Mid-Continent, 112
Superbowl, 1974, 189
Sweatt, Herman, 121
Sweeney-Coombs Building, 37, **37**

T
Taft, Paul, 109, 112
Taub, Ben, 86, 139
Telegraph and Texas Register, 16, **18**, 19
Telephone exchange, first, 33
Tenneco Building, 188, **195**
Tennessee Gas Transmission Co., 94
1010 Lamar, 165
Terry, Benjamin F., 23, 28
Terry's Texas Rangers, 23
Texaco, 55, 112, 170, 171, 173

Texaco Heritage Plaza, 173
Texas (ship), **180**, 181
Texas A and M University, 179
Texas Air Control Board, 143
Texas Childrens' Foundation, 104
Texas Childrens' Hospital, 104
Texas Commerce Bank, 81, 172
Texas Commerce Tower, 160, 164, 165
Texas Commission for the Arts, 186
Texas Co., 51, 61
Texas Cyclone (rollercoaster), 190, **202**
Texas Declaration of Independence, 11
Texas Eastern Transmission Co., 94, 104, 150, 175
Texas Greys, 23
Texas Highway Commission, 168
Texas Highway Department, 128
Texas International Airline, 170
Texas League, 77
Texas Limited, 175
Texas Medical Center, 63, 99, 104, 111, 139, 162, 172, 183, 188, **194**, **196**, **199**
Texas Municipal League, 120
Texas National Bank, 81
Texas National Guard, 28
Texas Natural Resources Conservation Commission, 185
Texas Parks and Wildlife Department, 181
Texas Racing Commission, 181
Texas Rangers, 173
Texas Rocket (train), 87
Texas Southern University, 108, **108**, 121, 124, 147
Texas State University for Negroes, 108 121
Texas Turnpike Authority, 167
Texas Water Pollution Control Board, 138
Texas White House, **14**, 15
"The Broken Obelisk" (sculpture), 153, **153**
The Hospital (book), 140
The Houston Post, 37
"The Last American City," 3
The Raven (book), 7
Third Ward, 17
Thomas, Albert, 86, 87, **87**, 127, **127**, 129, 136, 140
Thomas, Lera, 146
Thompson, Thomas, 59, **59**, 73

Tidewater Associated, 112
Tinsley, Eleanor, 165
T. M. Bagby (ship), 39
Tomball, 6
Toronto Sun, 37, 171
Tranquility Base, 137
Tranquility Park, 163, 188, **192**
Transco Tower, 166, 188, **192**, **195**
Trinity River Authority, 142
Trolley cars, 23
Tuam Avenue Baptist Church, 52
Tunnel system, 163, **163**
Turner, Sylvester, 184, 185
Turning Basin, completed, 51, 58
2016 Main, 143
Two Houston Center Building, 156

U
Union Baptist Association, 131
Union National Bank, 53
Union occupation, 23
Union Station, 54, 157
United Bank, 173
United Bank Plaza, 168
United Gas, 77, 154
United States Football League, 170
United Way, 66
University of Dallas Medical Department, 99
University of Houston, 86, 89, **89**, 112, 140, 155, 172, 179
Cougars, 190, **202**
University of Houston, Downtown, 183, **183**
University of Houston School of Hotel and Restaurant Management, 89, **89**
University of St. Thomas, 93, 103, 105, **105**, 153
University of Texas, 88, 99
University of Texas Law School, 121
University of Texas Medical School, 63, 150
U.S. Customs Building, 58, 60, **60**
USS Houston, 78, 80, **80**, 94
USS Houston II, 95
U.S. Steel, 143

V
Valenti, Jack, 142
Vance, Nina, 103, 106, **106**, 149

Veterans Administration Hospital, 103, 184, **185**
Voting Rights Act, 164, 185

W
Walgreen's, 123
Warehouse conversions, 182, **182**
Warnash, John, 11
Warner Cable, 163
Warwick, Gary, 181, **181**
Warwick Apartment Hotel, 77
Warwick Hotel, 130, **130**, 138, 188
Washburn, Harry A., 103
Washburn Tunnel, 103
Washington, Craig, 175
Washington County, 24
Washington on the Brazos, 4, 11, 16
Watergate, 156, 157
Water pollution, 155
Water system, beginning, 29
Watson, Elizabeth, 176, **177**
Webb, James, 136
Webster, Frederick Leon, 79
Weingarten Realty Co., 73
Weingarten's, 123
Weiss, H. C., 62
Welch, Louis, 114, 116, 120, 142, 146, 155, 156, 177, 184, **184**
Wesley, Carter, 121
West, Jim, 66
West Ranch, 129
Western Bank, 173
Western Union, 161
Westmoreland, Jim, 177
Westside airport proposal, 171
Wharton, Clarence, 66
Wheeler Avenue Baptist Church, 123

White, Hattie May, 122, **122**
White, Mark, 168
White flight, 147
White Oak Bayou, 6
Whitmire, Kathy, 164, 167, 173, 175, 177, 184, **184**, 185
Wilkins, Horace, 87
Williams, Beneva, 123
Wilson, George, 12
Wilson, James T. D., 27
Wilson, Robert, 6, 7, 12, 27
Wilson, Welcome, 131, **131**
Wilson, Woodrow, 20, 58
Wood, Robert E., 101
Woodlands, The, 153
Woolworth's, 123
World Hockey Association, 155
World Trade Center, 134
World War I, 28
Wortham, Gus, 120, 189
Wortham Foundation, 188
Wortham Theater, 172, **204**, 207
Wyatt, Oscar and Lynn, 73
Wyndham-Warwick Hotel, 175

Y
Yates, Jack, 152
Yellow fever, 14, 23, 34
"Yellow Rose of Texas" (song), 6
Youngblood, Rufus, 131, **131**

Z
Zimmerman, Eddie, 74
Zindler, Marvin, 108, **109**
Zoning, 186
Zoning elections, 78
Zoo, 190, **201**